The Great Education Decision

Learning From the Past to Give Our Children an
Eternal Future

Isaac B. Moffett

DEDICATION

This is a dedication to all those before us who sounded the alarm against ungodly education. History has proven they were right all along.

CONTENTS

Section 1: Prevailing Worldviews

Section 2: Christian Curriculum Framework

Section 3: Plan of Action

ACKNOWLEDGMENTS

With an endeavor such as this one, there are always far more people who played a role in its completion than can be acknowledged. Even if I tried, I know I will still miss some, but there are just a few individuals I must mention.

First and foremost, I must give thanks to and acknowledge God for giving me life and for sustaining it, for providing me the mind to do what I do. All glory belongs to Him and Him alone.

Second, I must thank my wife for her encouragement and her sacrifice while I isolated myself in my office for many months. It is doubtful I would be able to do any of what I do without your support.

And I must thank my kids, Brianna and Brandon for their patience (most of the time) for not being available during the writing process. Now let's go fishing!

~Dad

FORWARD

Very few subjects are as important in our day as the issue of education. The future of eternal souls are at stake, and we must learn to think Biblically about the training and instruction of children. The Great Education Decision is an educational insider's look at the contrasting worldviews and philosophies that war against each other in the great battle for hearts and minds. This book engages the important task of learning to take every thought about education captive, and make it obedient to Christ. I applaud Isaac Moffett for this well-argued and well-reasoned thesis.

~Israel Wayne-
Author of *Full Time Parenting: A Guide to Family-Based Discipleship* and *Homeschooling from a Biblical Worldview.*

www.IsraelWayne.com
www.ChristianWorldview.net/blog

INTRODUCTION
By
Ray Fournier

Prepare to be informed and awakened as Isaac Moffett, host of *The Great Education Struggle Podcast*, exposes the prevailing anti-Christian philosophies of our culture, lays the foundation for an education that imparts a Biblical worldview, and introduces parents to a God centered (theocentric) classical liberal arts framework for education as a way to maximize the intellectual development and provide a truly biblical Christian education for our children. In *The Great Education Decision*, Isaac Moffett uses his extensive knowledge of education gained academically while earning a Master's of Science in Educational Leadership, a Post-Bachelor's of Arts Secondary Teacher Certification in Social Studies and History, a Bachelors of Arts in Social & Behavioral Science, and an Associate Degree in Secondary Education as well as knowledge gained from his independent study of God's Word and his experience as the principle founder of Nampa Classical Academy (NCA) to help Christian parents transition from public education to an authentic, biblical Christian education.

Whether you are a Christian parent who is fleeing the public schools due to Common Core or an experienced Christian schooler or home-schooler, *The Great Education Decision* will enlighten and enrich your understanding of our culture's anti-Christian philosophies imparted to our children by deliberate public school indoctrination. These philosophies are so widely taught by public school curriculums and the media that they have succeeded in insidiously infiltrating our churches and as a result, many Christian school and home-school curriculums. This means that even if you are a Christian school parent or home-schooler, you might still be unknowingly passing on these anti-Christian philosophies to your children. Reading *The Great Education Decision* will help you detect anti-Christian philosophies in "Christian" curriculums and learn how to make the wisest, God honoring educational decisions for your children.

Section 1: Prevailing Worldviews will give you a "Cliffs Notes" version of the six main anti-Christian philosophies that make up the dominant secular worldview of modern America. This section is very useful for anybody who doesn't have the time to take a college level course in philosophy. It is essential information for making your very own great education decision that is well organized and succinct in its presentation.

Section 2: Christian Curriculum Framework lays down the foundation of every authentically biblical Christian curriculum, the Word of God, by making the case for Sola Scriptura and the supremacy of scripture in education. This section was so inspirational to me that I couldn't help but copy down quote after quote for later use.

In *Section 3: Plan of Action* Isaac Moffett utilizes his extensive knowledge of a God centered (theocentric) classical liberal arts framework and pedagogy to introduce parents to a biblical Christian liberal arts education. In this section Isaac makes a case for utilizing the biblical Christian liberal arts approach to impart a purely biblical Christian worldview while maximizing our children's intellectual development so they may become leaders in their future families, communities, and the nation. This short 145 page book will be invaluable in helping you to make your very own great education decision.

Besides the educationally important and God honoring information in this book, for me, the biggest reason to continue reading is the genuine Christian character of the author. Isaac Moffett is not just a highly educated expert in the field of education; he is a courageous soldier for Christ. He is driven out of a deep love for God and Christian families to fight for our children and the glory of God in the battle field of education even if it means the loss of his career, reputation, and intense persecution. He has clearly demonstrated his character during his three year legal battle with the state of Idaho that included the closing of Nampa Classical Academy (NCA) due to Isaac's insistence on using the Bible as one of his official textbooks for history and literature, as well as when he came to my aid during my own time of persecution for the cause of Christ.

Continue reading and prayerfully consider what this genuine brother in Christ has to say. Prepare to be informed and awakened!

~Ray Fournier is a 15 year veteran of the public schools and author of *Education Reformation,* a book that presents a gospel-centered, Great Commission focused case against public education and encourages Christian parents to provide for their children a Biblical Christian education. **(www.EducationReformation.org)**

PREFACE

We live in a world that seems to be completely upside down. What once was good, true, and beautiful no longer is, and what once was seen as bad, false, and ugly now is viewed as good. Moreover, as time goes on, this phenomenon continues to grow exponentially. Many parents are concerned and have decided to withdraw their children from traditional brick and mortar public schools. Reasons cited are academic; for others, its safety. In an effort to find relief from the ills they are experiencing, parents move to public virtual charter schools, and others choose private schools. Then there are those who choose to homeschool. While there is an increasing number of self-proclaimed secular homeshoolers, the vast majority of homeschoolers have decided to include some element of biblical education as part of their academic instruction.

The one thing most parents do not do, regardless of their educational choice, is deliberately consider the worldview in which they live and, in turn, the worldview in which their chosen educational option will expose their children to. Arguably, most parents who choose private Christian schools think the total school program is Christian, but seldom do they say biblical Christian. After all, it has Christian in the name, and they use well-known Christian publishers for their curriculum. I even hear it said something like this: "Mrs. Jones teaches there, and I know she is a Christian." I do not doubt anyone's sincerity but what they never seem to look into or understand is that a school that has Christian in its name, uses Christian publishers for their curriculum, and employs "Christian" teachers, provides no assurance whatsoever the total school program consist of a biblical, Christian worldview. The same issues exist with the homeschool option. As Christian parents we must be deliberate in our educational choices and carefully examine the curriculum that we choose to educate our children with. The fact is that whenever learning material is presented, you are introducing something that has been influenced by a worldview. As a result, if you are a Christian parent, it is your responsibility to make a deliberate educational choice to impart a purely biblical, Christian worldview to your children.

Parents must examine the philosophical worldviews of each component of their education program. This inspection must occur whether or not the curriculum is from a Christian publisher, including homeschool curriculum. It is even more important now with the fundamental transformation of America through the implementation of the Common Core State Standards (CCSS) as evident by the majority of Christian publishers having capitulated and joined those in the CCSS camp to one degree or another.

The principles by which believers live are absolutely opposed to the principles by which unbelievers live. The real difference between theocentric education and that of public and most private schools, including many homeschool curriculum, must be traced back to the curriculum's ultimate source of truth.

Biblical Christians believe that mankind originally lived in the light of the revelation of God and that in Christ, revealing truth through His Word, man is in principle restored to the true light of God. In a biblical, Christian worldview the living God, our Creator, Redeemer, and Author of the Bible is not only the ultimate source of truth but also the standard of truth itself. On the other hand, every other worldview in one way or another explicitly or implicitly denies the God of the Bible as the source of all reality and the measure of all truth. There is, in fact, no neutral ground in education or elsewhere. Nothing can be taught apart from some religious orientation. If we want a God-centered and authentic biblical Christian education, we must completely sever ourselves from the educational philosophy that surrounds us all. While I wish to be positive and constructive (and I will be in the following chapters) and share with you how to make what I call, the great education decision to impart a biblical, Christian worldview to your children through your educational choices, I cannot be just positive and constructive due to the world of sin in which we live.

No Christian individual or organization can be positive and constructive until they have been negative and destructive. To deny or ignore the prevailing toxic worldviews that our children are being indoctrinated with in most educational situations is to deny or ignore reality itself, so please hang in here as I attempt to clearly explain the antitheses in worldviews we absorb with every breath we take. This small book is not intended to be a definitive declaration of the subject, but it is meant to awaken parents to the influences we have all become a part of and, therefore, have become blind to its effects and then to learn from the past in order to provide for our children an eternal future.

This book is not about CCSS, Christian schools, or publishers directly, but about what it means to have a biblical Christian curriculum framework. This book has many flaws in it, but it is my hope that, in spite of these flaws, readers will be able to look beyond them and glean from its content. Furthermore, it is my desire to provide fellow Christians with a name to describe what you have seen around you — a simple explanation for the strange world in which we live. Moreover, I hope to communicate that you are not alone in an era where darkness continues to encroach upon our nation and, in particular, upon our children. I hope it will provide reassurance to those who have already chosen a theocentric education and a road map back for those who have taken a different turn and are trying to find the way back for their children.

SECTION 1[1]

PREVAILING WORLDVIEWS

---

[1] Section 1 comes from research from different sources including a lecture given by Dr. R.C. Sproul. It wasn't until after I had written my first draft that I realized that his lecture has been transcribed into R.C. Sproul, *Lifeviews: Make a Christian Impact on Culture and Society.* (Grand Rapids, MI: Fleming H. Revell,1997). While I have

POST-CHRISTIAN AMERICA

For the biblical Christian parent, the current culture we live in clearly demonstrates Isaiah's warning, "Woe to those who call evil good and good evil, who put darkness for light and light for darkness, who put bitter for sweet and sweet for bitter!"[2] But his warning should not be a surprise, for there is a real antithesis between the biblical Christian view of the world and the way the non-believer views this world. You can see this when you ask a nonbeliever what he thinks the purpose of man is. The way we understand ultimate meaning is referred to as a worldview. Simply stated, a worldview is "a construct that, like eyeglasses, is the lens through which we interpret reality and make our everyday decisions."[3] The American Heritage® Dictionary describes one's worldview as "the overall perspective from which one sees and interprets the world; a collection of beliefs about life and the universe held by an individual or a group."[4]

Every human being who ever lived, lives today, and will ever live had, has, and will have a worldview which has been shaped by the culture in which they live(d). We all are bathed in the prevailing worldview of our culture, and this worldview shifts over time.

The Apostle Paul warned us of this when he wrote to the Roman believers, "Do not be conformed to this world ..."[5] He understood the prevailing pagan worldview in the Roman

[2] Isaiah 5:20.

[3] R.C. Sproul. "Secularism." (*Ligonier Ministries*, n.d,). Accessed June 2, 2014, http://www.ligonier.org/learn/devotionals/secularism.

[4] "Worldview." *The American Heritage® Dictionary of the English Language, Fourth Edition, 2003. Accessed* June 2, 2014 from http://www.thefreedictionary.com/worldview.

[5] Romans 12:2.

culture and warned fellow believers not to live, and, in fact, warned not to even think like nonbelievers for he told his readers to "renew their mind."[6] In other words, change the way you think. Think like Christians, not like unbelievers.

His instructions clearly indicate action from us. We must be active participants in nonconformance to the prevailing worldview of our culture. Now please do not take it further than I intend. We are called to live in the world, but we are also called to be distinct, to be holy.[7]

So how does this apply to the education of our children? I'm glad you asked. We must understand the times in which we live and be able to identify all worldviews that are not compatible with the worldview of Christ. As you will soon see, if you cannot recognize the antithesis worldviews in the school, teachers, and curriculum your children are exposed to, you may well be unwittingly bathing your children in the world we are not to be conformed to.

At this point, we must examine, albeit at a very elementary level, the dominant worldviews we all have been influenced by in order to see how our curriculum and instruction should look in accordance to a biblical worldview. Yes, that does mean we must become students, and students of philosophy at that.

Though we distinguish between laity and clergy within the Christian leadership structure, it is clear that every Christian is a missionary. The Bible instructs all of us believers to be missionaries in our own country, in our own sphere of

---

[6] Romans 12:2.

[7] 1 Peter 1:16; Leviticus 11:44, 45, 19:2, 20:7; Isaiah 35:8.

influence.[8] But for a missionary to be effective, the missionary must know the language and the culture of the society he or she lives in, as well as Bible content. My previous statement is even more relevant in post-Christian America, for America can no longer be assumed to be a Christian culture. Before you start with the "yeah buts," it must be said that:

> A post-Christian society is not merely a society in which agnosticism or atheism is the prevailing fundamental belief. It is a society rooted in the history, culture, and practices of Christianity but in which the religious beliefs of Christianity have been either rejected or, worse, forgotten ... At an emotional level, its Christian character explains why many agnostics and atheists nonetheless find Christian hymns suitable and comforting at occasions such as funerals and weddings. Intellectually, its dormant Christian beliefs—notably those about the nature of man—underpin our ideas on politics and foreign policy, as for instance on human rights. Even the Enlightenment—which strong secularists like to cite as the foundation of Western liberal polities—is an extension of Christianity as much as a rejection of it. In short, though much of what Christianity taught is forgotten, even unknown,

---

[8] Matt. 28:19. "It is important to note that Christ's commission to go and make disciples is given to the entire church, not just to individual Christians. It is popular to view the Great Commission as a command for every individual Christian to be involved in evangelism. And some missions advocates have claimed that unless you have a specific calling to stay home, you must become a cross-cultural missionary in obedience to the Great Commission. As well-intentioned as these viewpoints may be, they miss the mark when it comes to putting Christ's command in the context of the New Testament's teaching on the body of Christ" (Karl Dahlfred, "How Shall We 'Go.'" *Tabletalk Magazine,* [Sanford, FL: Ligonier Ministries, Inc., April 1, 2014]).

by modern Europeans and Americans, they nonetheless act on its teachings every day.[9]

Doesn't that speak of America in the twenty-first century? Now that we live in a post-Christian society, we must not allow the pendulum to swing the other way and claim we live in a pagan country, for a pagan culture has not been introduced and influenced by Christianity. This clearly has not been the case in America or western civilization. Today we live in a secular environment—a post-Christian phenomenon.

We also have to take into account that we do not live in a monolithic culture and, because of these competing worldviews, Christians must be aware of the dominant system operating in our culture. Today, besides biblical Christianity, there are arguably six major schools of theoretical thought operating in our society:

Existentialism	Positivism
Humanism	Pluralism
Pragmatism	Hedonism

All six of these worldviews can be summed up in one word: secularism. But, what is secularism? An "ism" is a school of thought, a value system, a philosophy, a worldview. The word "secular" comes from the Latin *saeculum*, meaning "world." Put it together and we have secularism, the idea that all of life must be judged by today's values. In the study of history, we call that presentism.

---

[9] John O'Sullivan, "Our Post-Christian Society: Christianity, Post-Christianity, and the Future of the West," *National Review Online,* December 14, 2013. Accessed June 14, 2014, http://www.nationalreview.com/article/366263/our-post-christian-society-john-osullivan.

The Bible concerns itself with long-range considerations, for God Himself is timeless, eternal-transcendent, and He looks at everything from an eternal perspective. We clearly see this in Genesis 1:1: "In the beginning, God created the heavens and earth."[10] At the core of Christianity, we must believe God is omniscient.[11] God considers everything under the auspices of the eternal, *Sub speci Aeternitatis.* Jesus reminds us that where He comes from is beyond time and space. He descends from the eternal realm, and His perspective is not for the now, but the eternal.[12]

He calls the Christian to live life in light of eternity. From a biblical worldview, what you do has eternal significance. The antithesis to the eternal perspective is the secularist's motto which can be summed up as "right now only counts right now." Philosophers call this *hic et nunc,* the philosophy of the "here and now."[13] This, of course, removes any eternal purpose for man or his existence. You clearly see this worldview at play all around us, particularly in advertising. Does "Living the high life," "This bud's for you," or "Just do it" ring a bell? What was the message being communicated to you and your children through those commercials?

From a biblical worldview, actions have a cause and a consequence. The consequence takes us to tomorrow and the next day through the last recorded syllable of recorded time. But for the Christian, there is no last syllable of recorded time. Our lives are forever.

---

[10] The Hebrew word used for God is *Elohim* which represents a plurality. This is the first mention of a trinity— God, Son, and Holy Spirit.

[11] Transcendent, outside of the time and space, eternal.

[12] John 8:21-30ff.

[13] "*Hic Et Nunc.*" Merriam-Webster.com. Accessed May 15, 2014. http://www.merriam-webster.com/dictionary/hic et nunc.

Now let's open the umbrella up and look at the six major strands of philosophical thought we consume and perhaps gorge ourselves on every day.

The prevailing worldview in America

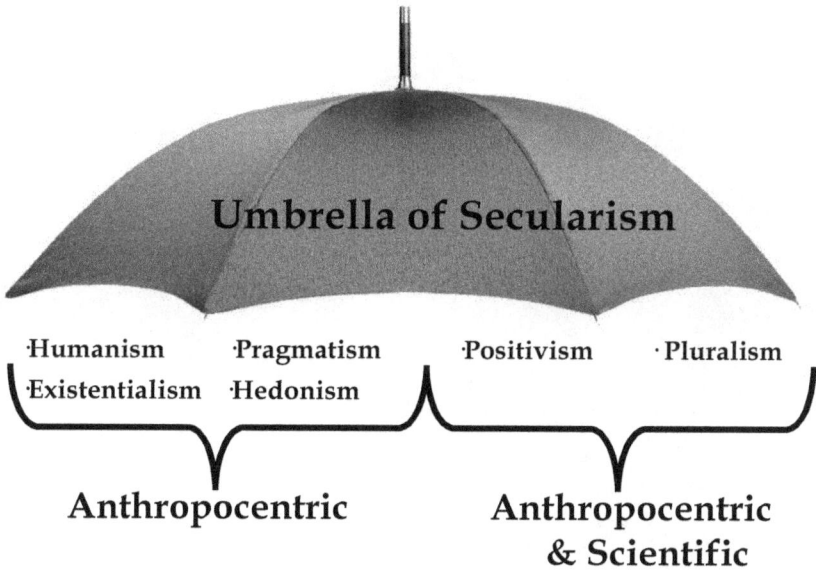

Umbrella of Secularism

·Humanism   ·Pragmatism   ·Positivism   · Pluralism
·Existentialism   ·Hedonism

Anthropocentric   **Anthropocentric & Scientific**

Notes

EXISTENTIALISM

Arguably, no philosophical system has affected twentieth-century America more than that of existentialism. The vast majority of people cannot define existentialism, but nonetheless, everyone encounters the influence of existentialism every day in every area of life.

In its most basic definition, existentialism is a philosophy about human existence. It views man not so much in terms of his mind or his soul, but of his will—his feelings. When was the last time someone asked you what you thought of this or that versus what you felt about this or that? Most likely, the "felt" question is what you are asked most often. Maybe it is the "felt" question you have most often asked. Today, we can thank existentialism for feelings having become the new standard of truth.

Existentialism has grown rapidly because its proponents have been brilliant and gifted men, such as Jean-Paul Charles Aymard Sartre, Albert Camus, Søren Aabye Kierkegaard, and Friedrich Wilhelm Nietzsche.[14] Another reason existentialism has gained such acceptance is that it dealt with human existence as opposed to abstract theories of epistemology.[15]

The formal existentialism movement began in the nineteenth century with theistic- and atheistic-supported varieties, supported by Kierkegaard and Nietzsche

---

[14] As a playwright and novelist, Sartre used his profession to influence the public towards existentialism; Camus used his novels to express his philosophical ideas; Kierkegaard used his poetic writing style to attract his readers; and Nietzsche used his gift of communication and writing to express his ideas.

[15] Branch of philosophy concerned with the nature and scope of knowledge and is also referred to as "theory of knowledge" ("Epistemology." *Merriam-Webster.com*. Accessed May 15, 2014, from http://www.merriam-webster.com/dictionary/epistemology.)

respectively. However, it wasn't really felt in America until after World War II. The destruction of the war, and even more so of the concentration camps all over Europe, moved many to fall into despair concerning humanity. Philosophers looked around and were astonished to see what man was capable of doing. This reality was enough to push the United States into agreeing to the establishment of the United Nations, whereas 20 years earlier the American people flat out rejected the same organization under the name of The League of Nations. Of course, this wasn't a mankind issue as much as it was a sin issue in a Genesis 3 world, but they failed to acknowledge this fact.

The atmosphere of the roaring 1920s crashed under the weight of the shadow of knowledge that man was capable of such evil. This feeling of despair found a root in the artist colonies such as Greenwich Village with the Beatnik movement, where they communicated some of the basic concepts of existentialism in their art. In fact, modern art has been the primary vehicle in transferring existential ideas.

The film and theater industry furthered these motifs. This theme boiled down to the idea that modern man is living in absence of God, and he is waiting and hoping God will show up. Hollywood brought a noticeable shift in plots and storylines. There are not many left who remember when Hollywood would tell a story of struggle, pain and death, yet always ended as a happy-ever-after story. Think of Roy Rogers, Jimmy Stewart, Gene Autry, James Arness, Lorne Greene, and the Lone Ranger. Oh how I miss those days of films ... but I digress. We all knew who the good guy was, even if he didn't have his white hat on. His character just oozed with nobility and virtue.

The existentialist theme brought in films of hopelessness. The black hat became the symbol of the good guy and the hero became the antihero. Remember Marlon

Brando and his motorcycle? John Wayne's Green Berets were no longer the good guys and were replaced with Catch-22 and M*A*S*H. Yes, Hawkeye and B.J. Hunnicutt were major vehicles in transmitting the existentialist ideas into our culture, to my great disappointment. Next time you watch, pay attention to the underlying themes. The ultimate meaningless of life was communicated by Atonini's *Blow Up* and the Jane Fonda's movie; *They Shoot Horses, Don't They?*

The Theater of the Absurd went so far as to demonstrate a new message that life has no meaning, there is nothing that brings the universe together in a coherent manner, and it was a movement away from rationality toward irrationality. This thought opened the door for other religious movements that embraced the existential principles, such as the American tradition of Zen Buddhism.

The central idea of existentialism is, as Sartre coined, "existence precedes essence." Traditionally, the search in philosophy was the quest for universals, for the unification of all the particulars of our daily lives. Sartre was not concerned with the essence of truth, but with the individual, the particular, with the concrete, not the abstract. He believed the individual counted, not the group, for if you are going to make sense of your life, it had to come from your own experience. The only valid conclusions came from one's personal experience. Man lived in this dimension only. There is no life beyond time and space; therefore, no eternity to worry about.

There are several major themes in existentialism. First, there is nothingness, coined as Nihilism.[16] Nihilism proclaims that there is no meaning to the human experience.

The second motif is that of despair and dread, which Hollywood films exploit all the time. The writers who champion this worldview will even use the words "despair" and "dread" in their writings to drive home this view. When life has no meaning and there is nothing before life or after, how can one not feel dreadful and be full of despair?

Camus went as far as believing and teaching that there was only one really serious philosophical problem and that is suicide.[17] If there is nothing before life and nothing after you die, why wouldn't suicide be just as viable an option as living? We have witnessed this play out with legislation and voter initiatives being passed to allow doctor-assisted suicide in several states. This debate was highlighted on November 1, 2014, when 29-year-old Brittany Maynard took a lethal dose of prescribed medication for the purpose of ending her own life under Oregon's Death with Dignity Act after contracting grade 4 glioblastoma. Belgium even extends the legalization

---

[16] Nietzsche is referred to as the father of Nihilism. Nihilism is a philosophy of despair that says there is no meaning to the human existence. There are no alternate values in life. The only meaning you can discover in this world is the meaning you determine for yourself. There is no transcendent meaning, only your preference. Human existence came from nothing and ends in nothing. "Nihilism." Merriam-Webster.com. Accessed May 15, 2014. http://www.merriam-webster.com/dictionary/nihilism. Also see Stephen Law, Julian Baggini, and Barry Loewer. *30-Second Philosophies: The 50 Most Thought-Provoking Philosophies, Each Explained in Half a Minute.* (New York: Fall River Press by arrangement with Ivy Press, 2009), p. 143.

[17] Ronald Aronson, "Albert Camus", *The Stanford Encyclopedia of Philosophy* (Spring 2012 Edition), Edward N. Zalta (ed.), Accessed May 15, 2014, from http://plato.stanford.edu/archives/spr2012/entries/camus/.

of suicide to children of any age.[18] How long before it comes to America?

Another theme is "angst" or anxiety—the undefined, faceless feeling inside of oneself. Martin Heidegger wrote *Being and Time*, which describes man as being thrown into the world.[19] Your life and your existence are defined by where you are—where you live. He preached that man was thrown into a world with nothing and is expected to carve out an existence between the poles of nothingness.[20]

The last major theme is that of freedom and autonomy in which there are no norms because there are no absolutes. The individual is free to do what he wants and is, in fact, responsible for doing what he wants. There is no right thing to do unless you want to do it. For a man with this worldview, like writers Ernest Hemmingway and Nietzsche, who look into the pit of despair, the black void of nothingness, he sees life as hopeless and meaningless.

Dr. R.C. Sproul[21] used the following syllogism to demonstrate this strange way of living in this world.

> Life is meaningless.
> We must face life with courage.[22]
> Our courage is meaningless.

---

[18] Charlotte McDondald-Gibson, "Belgium Extends Euthanasia Law To Kids." *Time,* February 13, 2014. Accessed on June 19, 2014, from http://time.com/7565/belgium-euthanasia-law-children-assisted-suicide.

[19] Martin Heidegger, *Being and Time.* (New York: Harper, 1962).

[20] Law, *at. el.,* "Heidegger's Nothing." *30-Second Philosophies*, 2009, pp. 150-51.

[21] Theologian and president of Reformation Bible College.

[22] Referred to as dialectical courage.

Nevertheless, man chooses not to surrender by seeking the safety of the group and its conventional values and institutions. Instead, he has the courage to exercise his own absolute freedom.[23] He takes sole responsibility for his actions.

It is important to note that those who have this worldview today will tell you they have the freedom to do what they want, but when actually taking reasonability provides no benefit to them, they are quick to lay blame elsewhere and dress themselves as a victim. We clearly see this play out with the youth revolution of the 1960s onward.

This worldview is the strongest example of secularism in our culture today. You and your children have been saturated in this way of thought. It permeates the textbooks, the arts, and sadly most sermons preached in American churches today. It is important to keep your eyes open for Existentialism as you strive to make the great education decision.

---

[23] Law, *at. el.*, "Sartre's Bad Faith." *30-Second Philosophies*, 2009, pp. 152-53.

Notes

HUMANISM

Now let's turn our attention to one of the two primary worldviews of America's public schools, and in many cases private schools. Humanism, often referred to as secular humanism, is an ancient philosophy and has undergone numerous changes, but it should not be confused with humanitarianism.

Humanism has its beginnings in ancient Greece by Protagoras. He established the foundation of humanism when he said, *"Homo mensura,"* or "Man is the measure" of all things. Not the character of God, not the being of God, but man. In other words, humanism is *anthropocentric, or* man-centered. Man becomes his own standard — the ultimate being, ultimate authority, and ultimate reality. It's all about man or shall we say, it's all about me? The antithesis of anthropocentric is *theocentric*, or God-centered. As you can see, there is a built-in conflict between these worldviews. Much like oil and water can never mix and become one or even complement each other, anthropocentric and theocentric worldviews can never be in the same room and be at peace with each other.

Earlier forms of humanism, known as theistic humanism, did acknowledge God's existence but limited His power, with His ability being relegated to the creation of the natural realm, but this religion came in through the view of naturalism,[24] not from a transcendent creator. The early humanist would agree there was a god, but they would also deny this god's supernatural involvement in the world he created. All through history, humanism has always presented itself as a purposeful alternative to Christianity.

---

[24] "The doctrine that scientific laws are adequate to account for all phenomena" (Naturalism. [n.d.]. Accessed June 27, 2014, from http://www.merriam-webster.com/dictionary/naturalism).

During the sixteenth century, a battle raged between Martin Luther and Desiderius Erasmus.[25] Erasmus is considered the Prince of Renaissance humanism.[26] Renaissance humanism, as taught by Erasmus, can be summed up as the idea that religion is just a part of your human experience. Again, you can see the anthropocentric view in this. Luther won the debate in the sixteenth century, but it was short lived. By the Enlightenment of the eighteenth century, humanism took a foot hold. But it wasn't until the nineteenth century that humanism and theology combined into what is known as "liberalism."[27]

Liberalism in theology is an attempt to reconstruct Christianity on a basis of naturalism. For example, liberal theologians and pastors removed all of the supernatural, such as creation, the plagues of Egypt, the virgin birth, and the resurrection of Christ. It was a clash between supernatural Christianity and those who only held to the social and ethical teachings of the New Testament. The theologians who held to the liberal belief did not believe in the virgin birth and resurrection of Christ. But doesn't this beg to question what

---

[25] Also known as Erasmus of Rotterdam.

[26] Referred to as "the crowning glory of the Christian humanists" (Kenneth Scott Latourette. *A History of Christianity*. [New York: Harper & Brothers, 1953], p. 661.). Erasmus coined the motto: *ad fontes*, "to the soure[s]." His encouragement to return to the original sources of Scripture brought about the *textus receptus* (Latin: "received text.") which in turn brought us the Greek New Testament, which the King James Bible was based upon.

[27] It is important to note this is not the same as classical liberalism which was a political philosophy and ideology belonging to liberalism in which primary emphasis is placed on securing the freedom of the individual by limiting the power of the government. The philosophy emerged as a response to the Industrial Revolution and urbanization in the nineteenth century in Europe and the United States. It advocates civil liberties with a limited government under the rule of law, private property rights, and belief in laissez-faire economic liberalism (Richard Hudelson. *Modern Political* Philosophy [M.E. Sharpe, Inc. Armonk, NY, 1990], pp. 37–38).

do you have left without the resurrection of Christ?[28] Why continue to participate in "Christianity," especially as a pastor?

Liberalism caused a shift from a personal supernatural redemption to a "social gospel" salvation through the social works we do, such as helping the poor. They didn't believe in the supernatural, but they did believe in the ethics or values of the New Testament and, because of this, argued they still had a viable ministry to carry out.

It was at this point that humanists and liberals became allies. Nineteenth-century humanists still saw religion as valuable. Not necessarily valid but useful, for it called men to high virtues. These virtues can be summed up as 1) compassion for the human condition, 2) service to mankind, 3) honesty, 4) industry and hard work, and 5) freedom and democracy. Christians held to all of these ideas and, therefore, they were congruent. Both camps agreed to disagree on the fundamental ideas of the Gospel in order to work together to help the poor, establish hospitals, orphanages, poorhouses, etc.

It is important to note that the humanists of the nineteenth century are not the same as those in the twentieth and twenty-first centuries. During the twentieth century, modern humanists became militant towards Christianity. You can clearly see this in the *Humanist Manifesto I, II, & III.* Their stated goal moved from cooperative endeavors to the total eradication of Christianity. This clearly can be seen in John J. Dunphy's essay published in *The Humanist*:

> The battle for humankind's future must be waged and won in the public school classroom by teachers who correctly perceive their role as the proselytizers of a new faith: a religion of

---

[28] 1 Corinthians 15:12-19.

humanity—utilizing a classroom instead of a pulpit to carry humanist values into wherever they teach. The classroom must and will become an arena of conflict between the old and the new —the rotting corpse of Christianity, together with its adjacent evils and misery, and the new faith of humanism.[29]

Early twentieth-century academics held to this belief and, in fact, believed Christianity hindered the progress of man. As a replacement to the Gospel of Jesus Christ, they believed and taught that the only way to cure the world of its ills, especially the evil of man, was to change the world through schooling. Today, this is commonly referred to as social engineering. One man in particular held this belief, and his name was John Dewey, the father of the modern American education system. His pedagogic creed can be summed up by his own words:

I believe that education, therefore, is a process of living and not a preparation for future living; I believe that education is the regulation of the process of coming to share in the social consciousness; and that adjustment of individual activity on the basis of this social consciousness is the only sure method of social reconstruction … I believe that every teacher is a social servant set apart for the maintenance of proper social order and the securing of the right social growth. I believe that in this way the

[29] John J. Dunphy. "A New Religion for the New Age." *The Humanist*, (January/February1983), p. 26.

teacher always is the prophet of the true God and the usher in of the true kingdom of God.[30]

Clearly, there is an obvious struggle between Christianity and humanism. Humanism borrows from Christian ethics while denying accountability to its source, Christ. The noble ideals of humanism have no rational foundation. Christianity thrives on "principles," the humanist on "preferences," and the principal vehicle for the dissemination of humanist philosophy is the public school system. Twentieth-century humanists understood this as evident when humanist leader Charles F. Potter wrote:

> With the exclusion of God and his moral principles, … during the last decades, humanists have been very successful in propagating their beliefs. Their primary approach is to target the youth through the public school system, thus education is thus a most powerful ally of humanism, and every American school is a school of humanism. What can a theistic Sunday school's meeting for an hour once a week and teaching only a fraction of the children do to stem the tide of the five-day program of humanistic teaching?[31]

Think about that for a minute or two. Let it sink in. Potter wrote this in 1930 and he reports this indoctrination

---

[30] John Dewey. *The Early Works of John Dewey, Vol. 5: My Pedagogic Creed* (Jo Ann Boydston, Ed.), (Southern Illinois University Press, 1972), pp. 84-85. Also see Stella Van Patten Henderson. *Introduction to Philosophy of Education.* (Chicago: The University of Chicago Press, 1947), p. 208.

[31] Charles Frances Potter. *Humanism: A New Religion.* (New York: Simon and Schuster, 1930), p. 128.

had been going on for decades prior. What can Sunday school and a few minutes of meaningful conversation with your child(ren) do to hold back the tide of indoctrination?[32] Spoiler alert: Jesus has already answered this for us in Luke 6:40 "A disciple is not above his teacher, but everyone when he is fully trained will be like his teacher."

Humanism could only emerge from a society that had previously been committed to its meaningful origin in a meaningful destiny of the human race. Humanism has rejected Christianity not realizing they have rejected the very foundation for the humanity they seek to elevate. We must ask the humanists, "If I come from nothing, if I'm going to nothing, I am nothing, then why should I care who sits in the back of the bus, or who gets healthcare? Give me one reason why you should treat one human being with dignity other than simply he has to preference that I do?" You see, humanism is based on sentimentality. It is in anthropology that has no support.

There is a great deal more that can be said about the humanistic indoctrination that is intentionally being carried out in America's public schools and its effects on our children's eternal future. But what has already been said, should be sufficient to eliminate public education as an option when striving to make the great education decision.

---

[32] The average American parent spends 38.5 minutes per week in meaningful conversation with their child. What chance does your child have attending public school? (Lisa Belkin. "Don't turn off the TV week." *New York Times, Parenting Blog*, April 21, 2009. Accessed June 27, 2014, http://parenting.blogs.nytimes.com/2009/04/21/dont-turn-off-the-tv-week/?_php=true&_type=blogs&_r=0).

Notes

PRAGMATISM

Now let's move on to another view that has greatly affected both public, private, and homeschool curricula. Unlike all other philosophical movements which were transported from Europe to America, pragmatism was birthed right here in America and reflects the American culture. Have you ever heard of Yankee Ingenuity, also known as the "can do" attitude of America? If pragmatism had a motto, it would be "Where there's a will there's a way."

You can see this in Harvey Cox's *The Secular City*[33] which evaluates pragmatism as being the dominant influence in producing the American lifestyle. Interesting point. Notice Cox's play on Augustine's *City of God* when he titles his own book, but I digress. He points out that pragmatists don't think in terms of ultimate or religious questions. The spirit of pragmatism is the spirit of problem solving. Additionally, the pragmatist is either skeptical or agnostic about man's ability to discover ultimate truth. As a formal philosophy, pragmatism proceeds from a prior skepticism of metaphysics[34] or theology and looks at life from the perspective of naturalism.

There is a point of distinction between pragmatism and Christianity, however. Romans chapter 1 paints a bleak picture of the man who will not consider God. What you choose to believe or not to believe greatly affects your actions, and people act in accordance to what they believe.

[33] Harvey Gallagher Cox. *The Secular City: Secularization and Urbanization In Theological Perspective*, (New York: Macmillan. 1965).

[34] "A division of philosophy that is concerned with the fundamental nature of reality and being and that includes ontology, cosmology, and often epistemology" ("Metaphysics." [n.d.]. Accessed June 4, 2014 http://www.merriam-webster.com/dictionary/metaphysics). See Metaphysics (n.d.). Accessed June 4, 2014, from http://www.merriam-webster.com/concise/metaphysics).

Pragmatism is a theory of truth, and practicality is a test of this truth. Since there is no transcendent truth for the pragmatic, truth is what works. As a result, pragmatism is highly subjective. As William James wrote, "The truth is the name of whatever proves itself to be good in the way of belief ..."[35]

Pragmatists are anthropocentric for their truth is man-made.[36] Pragmatism is the exact opposite of principle-based decision making. Godly principle and precept decision making is its antithesis.

Pragmatism really was cultivated by three philosophy students at Harvard during the late nineteenth century. These men, Charles Peirce, William James, and Oliver Wendell Holmes Jr[37] (and later John Dewey), became the leading spokesmen and promoters for the philosophy of pragmatism in American culture, although Dewey preferred to call it instrumentalism or experimentalism.[38]

Out of their denial of transcendent norms, these men began to look for an alternative approach (they had to fill the void they created) to discover the purpose of man and the meaning of life. Since they believed they could not know transcendent truth, values, and norms (in other words, they did not believe in a transcendent creator), they decided the

---

[35] William James. *Pragmatism*. (New York: Longmans, Green & Co., 1907), p. 76. Dewey was heavily influenced by James and, as a result, James' views were assimilated into the modern education pedagogy through Dewey's progressive model.

[36] Henderson, *Introduction to Philosophy of Education*, p.225, 245.

[37] Holmes became an Associate Justice of the United States Supreme Court from 1902-32. Think about how this worldview has influenced and shaped court rulings, and our national direction.

[38] Henderson, *Introduction to Philosophy of Education*, pp. 225-27 & William James.*The Varieties of Religious Experience Study in Human Nature*. (New York: The Modern Library, 1902), pp. 434-35.

only way they could know what was right was through experimentation. Truth became relative and subjective. If your choice worked favorably for you, then the action you took was the correct action for you. It does not matter if the same choice caused problems for someone else. If it does, then that choice was not true or correct for them.

Historically, there have been several key criticisms of pragmatism. Like I have already stated, pragmatism is utterly subjective. Second, it tends to focus on short-term consequences, and problem solving often leads to more problems for example, self-medicating with alcohol or illegal drugs. For a short time, the pain you are trying to find relief from is subdued, but this cure causes many more problems as consequences later on.

You can see this play out in government today. Government leaders see we have a jobless problem. Congress finances billions of dollars in foreign loan monies to put people to work. We will deal with the nation's ability to pay the loans off, or the lack thereof, in the years ahead. The problem in front of us is "solved" for we are told that those people who were out of work are now working. The pragmatist never looks at the long-term problem when deciding how to solve short-term issues. We use to call this, kick-the-can out on the playground.

Pragmatism focuses on what is expedient. Like the high priest, Caiaphas, who determined that it was expedient for one man to die for the sake of the nation,[39] pragmatism makes a casualty of any concept of justice. There is no place for pragmatism to enquire what is right. If something is true for you, if it helps you get along in life, if it helps you cope and succeed, then it's practical and true.

---

[39] John 18:14

As William James wrote, "There is nothing more to the nature of truth than this."[40]

Another point of criticism is that it is anti-intellectual and rejects first principles and ideas. James asserts that what matters are not the first principles but the final ones: the fruit of the idea. As noted, he used the concept of an idea's "cash value"—what it accomplishes—as its truthfulness. Peirce believed that if an idea could not be used in a particular situation, then it had no meaning and was worthless. James links pragmatism to other philosophic tendencies of the nineteenth century, such as nominalism (appeals to particulars, not universals), utilitarianism (emphasis on the practical aspects), and positivism (disdain for verbal solutions and metaphysical abstractions).

Pragmatism is one of the major reasons for the near collapse of classical and Christian liberal arts education for the past 100 years. Embracing the philosophy of pragmatism and its educational belief system, known as progressivism, became the antithesis of a classical and Christian education. In fact, progressivism is embedded in nearly every curriculum framework, regardless of whether it is secular or parochial, including homeschool curricula. This clearly can be seen with the hyper focus on getting good grades in school which in turns lets you get into college which leads to getting a good job, and thus happy ever after. The real message here is that by being obedient and going to college, you will become a compliant widget maker. No focus, not even a mention of living a good and noble life. One exception would be that of authentic classical and Christian liberal arts curricula. These curricula are the antithesis, the antidote to progressive education and its subdivisions. (More on that later.)

---

[40] Cited in Law, *at. el.*, "James' Pragmatism." *30-Second Philosophies*, 2009, pp. 134-35.

Progressive education sees the school—both public and private—as an institution of social and societal change through its curriculum and instruction. We call this indoctrination and see it running rampant today in our public school system.

Progressive education replaces primary sources with textbooks, edited to meet the social change being sought after. When was the last time your child was required to read the complete, unabridged piece from the Western canon? Would you know if a piece of literature was a member of the Western canon?

Under the progressive education model, the role of the teacher changed to that of a facilitator, and the education program changed to that of being child centric.[41] This idea has been incorporated, at least in part, in those who homeschool under the name of "unschooling," and multiple intelligences as taught by Howard Gardner. In other words, the child becomes the center of the education experience, not the teacher or the ultimate truths being taught and, in turn, learned. Progressives believe the child must be free to explore their own "truth" and discover knowledge on their own. The teacher is discouraged not to direct her students to a stated lesson objective, for the child will decide to learn what he or she wants to learn.

By the 1940s, progressive education had become the dominant American pedagogy. In fact, all public schools in America had adopted and implemented this model which was coined as "modern education," and new teachers from the universities and "normal" schools were taught that the "old-fashioned" education was rigid, subject-centric, and authoritarian, but this new, modern way was flexible, child-centered, democratic, and progressive. Do any of these

---

[41] Common Core State Standards teacher editions referr to the teacher as facilitators.

adjectives sound familiar?

These modern educators rejected the idea that education was to improve the intellect and preserve western and American civilization through the study of the Great Books and traditional subjects, such as history, civics, English, science, and mathematics. They wanted schools that used experiences and projects instead of reading assignments. Activities were to be negotiated between teacher and students with an emphasis on cooperation versus competition.

The high school saw a dramatic change during this time period as well. By the late 1800s it became clear that the different strands of theoretical thoughts embraced by different groups had caused a major disunion in terms of education, and the major education designers believed that a unified, basic standardization of what all students need to learn and be able to do was needed for the country. Yes, the discussion for a national standard has been on the table for a long time! These people just don't give up.

To resolve this disharmony, the National Education Association formed the Committee of Ten in 1892. This group, made up of primarily those in higher education, returned with a recommendation that all high school students, regardless of their station in life or career path, should receive a liberal arts education made up of English, Greek/Latin, modern languages, mathematics, history/civics, and science.[42] Point of interest: these were the subjects taught to sons of freemen during the previous 2,000 years.

Twenty-one years later, the progressives now fully in charge of the teachers' colleges, the National Education Association created the Commission on the Reorganization of

---

[42] National Education Association of the United States. Committee of Ten On Secondary School Studies. *Report Of The Committee Of Ten On Secondary School Studies: With Respect Of The Conferences Arranged By The Committee.* (Published for the National Education Association by the American Book Co., 1894), pp. 53-54.

Secondary Schools (CRSE). After three years, this commission recommended abolishing the liberal arts program for a more social engineering design plan.[43] In their report, they recommended the following seven areas to be taught to all students:[44]

1. Health
2. Command of the fundamental processes
3. Worthy home-membership
4. Vocation
5. Citizenship[45]
6. Worthy use of leisure
7. Ethical character[46]

These subjects, in comparison to the Committee of Ten recommendations, were the courses taught to slaves for the past 2,000 years (in particular, the vocational training). They, of course, did not call them slaves, but workers. After all, the industrial society had emerged.

These educrats took Dewey's pragmatic ideas of education to such an extreme direction that, in 1938, Dewey rebuked these extremists when he wrote *Experience and Education*. Mr. Dewey, you should have known better; ideas have consequences.

---

[43] "The Cardinal Principles of Secondary Education." (1918.). Transcribed by Melissa Scherer. Accessed July 2, 2014 from www.3.nd.edu/~rbarger/www7/cardprin.html.

[44] *Ibid.*

[45] Democracy, not a constitutional republic.

[46] Remember, the humanist likes the NT ethics, just not the author. "The Cardinal Principles of Secondary Education." (1918.). Transcribed by Melissa Scherer. Accessed July 2, 2014 from www.3.nd.edu/~rbarger/www7/cardprin.html.

The main conflict between Christianity and pragmatism is the conflict between what is right and what is expedient. From a biblical worldview, all truth that works must be measured against the character and nature of God, not what I personally want or feel.

Take a look at the comparison chart based upon Jeanne S. Chall's book, *The Academic Achievement Challenge,* on the preceding page. Do you see your education? For those of you who send your children to either public or private schools, and for those of you who homeschool, which column do you see your child and yourself in?

Comparison[47]

Teacher-centered

Progressive Student-centered

Learning

Acquiring knowledge from the past and present and recognizing patterns that may occur in future; skills important for the individual and society; a core curriculum.

Learning based on the learner's interests; no required core curriculum; emphasis on integration.

Moral Development

Students learn right from wrong from their studies, from adult guidance, and from extra-curricular activities.

Morality develops from the individual's experience; it is best learned when not taught directly.

Curriculum

Core subjects are taught separately; history and geography are defined; explicit phonics used to teach reading.

Any subject can serve to develop problem-solving abilities and creativity; social studies combine history, sociology, geography, and anthropology.

---

[47] Jeanne S. Chall. *The Academic Achievement Challenge: What Really Works in the Classroom?* (New York: Guilford Press, 2000).

Work Habits

Students are expected to learn what is taught; students come to school with good and questionable habits and attitudes and must be helped to become good citizens and learners.

The best learning comes when students are interested in what they learn; therefore, teachers encourage students to follow their own interests in learning; students are assumed to have good habits.

Promotion

Promotion is largely by achievement; student may be retained if achievement is too low.

Social promotion is preferred; student is promoted with age group even if achievement is too low.

Teacher's Background

Education in subject matter being taught is preferred; of course, excellent teaching methods are also required to help students learn the content.

Teacher's mastery of subject matter is considered less important than an understanding of child and adolescent development.

Notes

POSITIVISM

Positivism, defined as a theory that theology and metaphysics are earlier imperfect modes of knowledge and that positive knowledge is based on natural phenomena and their properties and relations as verified by the empirical sciences,[48] emerged in Europe in the nineteenth century and is usually associated with August Comte. Comte was a scientist/philosopher with a vision for societal reformation. He envisioned a society dominated by scientific knowledge and believed one could use scientific methods when studying societies and re-engineer individuals in order to create these societies better.[49] He taught that the only real knowledge, and, in fact, the "supreme standard for judging the validity of human knowledge," was from sense-experiences—what we can learn from our five senses.[50]

Historically, humans have tried to find a unifying factor for all parts of life. For the biblical Christian, that unity is in God, but for Comte, there was a natural law for the universe, but not for society. As man progresses and matures, so does society. He believed man matured or "grew up" in three stages:

1. The *infantile stage*, where people seek religious answers;
2. The *philosophical stage,* based on more abstract reasoning—now without the need for religion;
3. The *scientific stage*, where man reaches maturity—far beyond needing religion.

---

[48] "Positivism." [n.d.]. Accessed June 3, 2014, from http://www.merriam-webster.com/dictionary/positivism).

[49] Henderson, *Introduction to Philosophy of Education*, p. 8.

[50] *Ibid.*

For Comte, the only absolute was that everything was relative. Comte's idea has been regarded as a religion without God.

Positivism led to logical positivism, which in turn led to analytical philosophy. Logical positivism holds that all meaningful statements are either analytic or conclusively verifiable, or at least confirmable by observation and experiment, and that metaphysical theories are therefore strictly meaningless. You may have heard this idea by its other name: logical empiricism. [51] Analytical philosophy seeks the solution of philosophical problems in the analysis of propositions or sentences and goes by its other name: philosophical analysis. [52]

A small group of thinkers known as the Vienna Circle[53] set out in the 1900s to eliminate the influence of metaphysics and religion on culture. The contribution of logical positivism was the Verification Principle, which states truth had to be verified empirically, or by the senses.[54] Since God could not be verified by the senses, the word "God" was meaningless.

---

[51] "Logical positivism" (n.d.). Accessed June 4, 2014, from http://www.merriam-webster.com/dictionary/logical positivism.

[52] "Analytic philosophy" (n.d.). Accessed June 4, 2014, from http://www.merriam-webster.com/dictionary/analytic philosophy.

[53] "Group of philosophers, scientists, and mathematicians formed in the 1920s that met regularly in Vienna to investigate scientific language and scientific method. It formed around Moritz Schlick (1882–1936), who taught at the University of Vienna; its members included Gustav Bergmann, Philipp Frank, Rudolf Carnap, Kurt Godel, Friedrich Waismann, Otto Neurath, Herbert Feigl, and Victor Kraft. The movement associated with the Circle has been called logical positivism. Its members' work was distinguished by their attention to the form of scientific theories, their formulation of a verifiability principle of meaning, and their espousal of a doctrine of unified science. The group dissolved after the Nazis invaded Austria in 1938" ("Vienna Circle." (n.d.). Accessed June 4, 2014, from http://www.merriam-webster.com/concise/vienna%20circle).

[54] "Verifiability Principle" (n.d.). Accessed June 4, 2014, from http://www.merriam-webster.com/concise/verifiability%20principle.

Ultimately, positivism divorces science from the whole realm of truth for it cuts science from its roots. It creates a universe without union and creates a sea of diversity with no possible foundation for meaning, and it cuts you off from meaning. Isn't this an awful heavy price for growing up?

Notes

PLURALISM

Let's turn our attention to the next strand competing for our minds. The basic tenet of pluralism[55] is that there is no ultimate unity to bring cohesiveness to our lives. We have particulars, but no universals; the relative, but not the absolute. This is the exact opposite of what our nation was founded upon: *E Pluribus Unum* — "out of the many, we become one." But with the idea of pluralism, we have become *E Pluribus Pluribus*, out of the many, we remain many, or can we say a hyphenated American at best? Modern man believes we are cut off from God, the transcendent point of unity, so all we are left with is plurality.

Plurality, as an "ism," means that there is no unity to life. There is nothing that brings it all together. Pluralism leads us to the twentieth-century buzz word of relativity[56] — the idea that there are different perspectives from which to consider everything and none of these different perspectives are wrong. If everything is relative, then nothing is concrete or ultimately true. Relativity leads necessarily to chaos, because there is no fixed reference point by which one measures or judges. If everything is relative, then there is no ultimate reference point. Have you noticed how this idea has permeated the public schools, the arts, and the American church today?

---

[55] "A theory that there are more than one or more than two kinds of ultimate reality" ("Pluralism." [n.d.]. Accessed June 3, 2014, from http://www.merriam-webster.com/dictionary/pluralism).

[56] "The belief that different things are true, right, etc., for different people or at different times" ("Relativism." [n.d.]. Accessed June 3, 2014, from http://www.merriam-webster.com/dictionary/relativism).

This is precisely where modern man finds himself today: with no ultimate fixed, stable, absolute reference point that defines his life or the meaning of his existence. If everything is relative, then he is relative and there is no substance to the meaning of his very life. Is there any wonder why people become depressed and commit suicide or other heinous crimes? With a worldview like this, why not?

Relativity is the very antithesis of Christianity for it leaves the church in total chaos, and it leaves a culture with purposes, but no purpose; truths, but no truth. Pluralism directly confronts Christianity. For example, people claim legal rights, but don't consider moral rights because morality has become relative. Just ask someone who calls themselves a pro-choice supporter, "Where did they get the right to murder an unborn human being—the government or God?" Christianity requires that all views be treated with tolerance, but not necessarily with validity. Pluralism objects to that.

The situation at the time of the flood was a situation of pure moral relativism where everyone did what was right in their own eyes. Sounds like a description of yesterday's news doesn't it? And when God destroyed all of that, the descendants of Noah came up with an idea, to do exactly the same thing! They were going to build a city. In their eyes, this city would endure, and the crowning achievement of this city would be a tower that reached up to heaven, the Tower of Babel.

If a curriculum that you are examining does not base its truth claims on the absolute truth of God's Word or its statements regarding morality on God's absolute moral law, throw it away!

Notes

HEDONISM

The last strand we will examine in brief is Hedonism. Hedonist holds to the doctrine that pleasure or happiness is the sole or chief good in life. [57] Hedonism defines the "good" or "true" in terms of "pleasure" and "pain." The highest good of man—the ultimate purpose of his being—is the enjoyment of pleasure and avoidance of pain. The hedonist seeks to increase pleasure and decrease pain.

This movement sprang from the ancient Greek school of the Cyrenaics. The Cyrenaics were crude hedonists as exemplified in the pictures of the ancient orgies. Hedonism actually became a religion where, through pleasure, man transcended to a higher experience of consciousness. Think of the reason for the temple prostitutes in ancient pagan cultures—it wasn't just about making money.

The Epicureans adopted a more moderate approach because of the "hedonistic paradox." They believed if one didn't find pleasure, one was frustrated. If one did, one became bored—both of which did not produce pleasure. The ultimate philosophical goal of the Epicurean was the achievement of the *atarachia* – the search for peace of mind.

Epicureans were not the only groups that were looking for peace of mind. The stoics settled for peace of mind, but through self-control. Epicureans looked for peace of mind by seeking the proper balance of hedonism, the optimum pleasure. Not too hot, not too cold … just right.

Hedonism, like the other philosophies, turns this philosophy into a philosophy of ultimates. Truth and goodness are determined by pleasure and pain. However, Christianity says up front that there will be pain along

---

[57]"Hedonism" [n.d.]. Accessed June 3, 2014, from http://www.merriam-webster.com/dictionary/hedonism.

the way. The hedonist declares Christ a fool for accepting unnecessary pain, but Christianity sees pleasure differently than does the hedonist.

The modern hedonist lets his "feelings" dictate his responses. We induce feelings artificially with drugs. Hedonism makes value judgments, producing a system of ethics which produces a behavioral pattern of morality. This is clearly evident, for we are a nation preoccupied with analyzing and altering our moods. This yet again another worldview that we must avoid when making the great education decision.

The great education decision begins with learning how to identify all of the worldviews in our culture that are at war with biblical Christianity so that we can reject every curriculum that contains these worldviews. This is then followed by learning how to impart a purely biblical worldview to our children with our educational decisions. Now that we can identify these worldviews, it is time for us to learn about the Christian curriculum framework.

Notes

SECTION 2

CHRISTIAN CURRICULUM FRAMEWORK

SOLA SCRIPTURA

Postmodernity, with its aversion to truth claims, has led both the modern world and the church to view the authority of the Bible differently. While lip service may still be given to the idea of biblical authority and Scripture, many professing Christians no longer view the Bible's authority as beyond criticism. However, *sola Scriptura,* the formal principle of the Protestant Reformation, is essential to genuine Christianity.

Sola Scriptura has to do with the sufficiency of Scripture as our supreme authority in all spiritual matters and life. It is not a claim that all truth of every kind is found in Scripture, but Scripture is a "more sure word," standing above all other truth in its authority and certainty. It is "more sure,"[58] according to the apostle Peter, than the information we gather firsthand through our senses."[59] Therefore, Scripture is the highest and supreme authority on any matter on which it speaks.

It is important to note that there are many important questions on which Scripture is silent. *Sola Scriptura* makes no claim to the contrary, nor does *sola Scriptura* claim that everything Jesus or the apostles ever taught is preserved in Scripture. It only means that everything necessary, everything binding on our conscience, and everything God requires of us is given to us in Scripture.[60]

---

[58] The English phrase "more sure" is the Greek word, βεβαιος or *bebaios*. It means to be "stable (literally or figuratively): firm, of force, steadfast, sure (Strong, James. "The New Strong's Expanded Dictionary of the Words in the Greek New Testament." In *The New Strong's Expanded Exhaustive Concordance of the Bible.* [Nashville, TN: Thomas Nelson, 2010]).

[59] 2 Peter 1:19 (KJV).

[60] 2 Peter 1:3.

Historical Background

It is imperative that *sola Scriptura* be viewed and exercised within the distinguishing features of the various epochs of redemptive history. For example, as a member of the new covenant community, I am not obligated to obey the prohibition against boiling a young goat in its mother's milk.[61] This prohibition belongs to a specific period of redemptive history. However, though this precise law has been revoked by the new covenant, its authority is not lessened by the fact that it has been surpassed by historical events within the Bible's own timeline.

Sola Scriptura was, therefore, established in principle with the giving of the law. For example, we see God telling Moses he was not allowed to "add to the word which I [God] am commanding you, nor take away from it, that you may keep the commandments of the LORD[62] your God which I command you."[63] God reiterates *sola Scriptura* to Moses when He tells Moses, "Whatever I command you, you shall be careful to do; you shall not add to nor take away from it."[64]

---

[61] Ex. 23:19; cf. Mark 7:19; & Rom. 14:14. At the Feast of Ingathering, as it is called in Ex. 23:16, the Jews were commanded to give thanks to God for the harvest they had received, and for their dependence upon Him for the next harvest. They were not to attempt to gain anything by the superstitious practices of the pagans, who, it is said, at the end of their harvest, boiled a kid goat in its mother's milk and sprinkled that pottage, in a pagan ritualistic way, upon their gardens and fields to make them more fruitful the following year. Israel was to abhor such foolish customs.

[62] Translated from the Hebrew word "Yahweh." Yahweh is God's unspeakable name, His memorial name, the name we are never to take in vain, the name protected by the Ten Commandments. The Jews would use the Tetragrammaton (YHWH) instead of spelling Yahweh's name completely, out of absolute reverence for His name. You may have also seen it written as G-d.

[63] Deut. 4:2.

[64] Deut.12:32.

Furthermore, God even told Moses' successor, Joshua:

> Be strong and very courageous; be careful to do according to all the law which Moses My servant commanded you: do not turn from it to the right or left, so that you may have success wherever you go. This book of the law shall not depart from your mouth, but you shall meditate on it day and night, so that you may be careful to do according to all that is written in it.[65]

If this principle of *sola Scriptura* was true in the Old Testament, can we not assume that it is all the more true in the New? Scripture clearly claims for itself this sufficiency — and nowhere more clearly than in 2 Timothy 3:15-17. Verse 15, "and how from childhood you have been acquainted with the sacred writings, which are able to make you wise for salvation through faith in Christ Jesus," affirms that Scripture is sufficient for salvation. Verse 16, "All Scripture is breathed out by God and profitable for teaching, for reproof, for correction, and for training in righteousness, ..." affirms the absolute authority of Scripture, which is *theopneustos,*[66] and profitable for our instruction. Verse 17 states, "that the man of God may be complete, equipped for every good work."

Being that Scripture is given by inspiration of God or, more accurately, is a product of God's out-breathing,[67] the Bible's authority is comprehensive and total, down to the very

---

[65] Josh. 1:7-8a.

[66] Translated from Greek as "God-breathed [out]."

[67] 2 Tim. 3:16, *theopneustos.*

words themselves.[68]

New Testament Example

Jesus Himself taught the apostles the principle of *sola Scriptura* as an unquestioning submission to the Scriptures. They understood that when Jesus commanded them to go into the entire world and proclaim the Gospel, they were to teach and demand compliance with "all that I have commanded you."[69] Moreover, Jesus demonstrated His belief in *sola Scriptura* when He responded to all three temptations by citing Scripture — Old Testament at that.[70]

Jesus, in the face of temptation, turned again and again to the Scriptures. "It is written," He said. That was all He needed to say. Furthermore, while the authority of the Bible rests on its own claim to be the Word of God, it also rests on Jesus' view of Scripture. Jesus makes it clear as to His view of *sola Scriptura* once again when, in John 10:35, He says, "Scripture cannot be broken." Taking just this line of thought — the reference in John 10:35 to the effect that 'Scripture cannot be broken' — we see Jesus' view of the authority of Scripture.[71] It is clear that *sola Scriptura* has an Old Testament and New Testament basis, and Jesus Himself makes it clear that all things necessary for salvation, faith, and life are taught in Scripture.

---

[68] 2 Tim. 3:15-17; Gal. 1:8-9; 2 Tim.2:2; "The whole counsel of God, concerning all things necessary for His own glory, man's salvation, faith and life, is either expressly set down in Scripture, or by good and necessary consequence may be deduced from Scripture: unto which nothing at any time is to be added, whether by new revelations of the Spirit, or traditions of men" (*The Westminster Confession of Faith*, 1647, Ch.1/Par. 6).

[69] Matt. 28:20.

[70] Matt. 4:4, 6, 7.

[71] In this case, the Old Testament, for the New Testament had yet to be written, for those who are New Testament only.

Hermeneutical Principles

Sola Scriptura also holds that the Bible has enough clarity that the ordinary believer can understand its meaning. The problem with most, however, is that they are hermeneutically illiterate, and those who aren't hermeneutically illiterate are often hermeneutically inconsistent. Furthermore, we must understand that Scripture incorrectly interpreted is no longer God's Word. Jesus proves this with His confrontation with Satan in the wilderness.[72] The authority in all that the Bible teaches assumes a valid and consistent hermeneutic interpreting of the variety of genres contained in Scripture.[73]

For example, there must be a clear appreciation of the difference between the descriptive and the prescriptive. While members of the post-Pentecost church in Jerusalem relinquished their rights to private ownership and sold all of their goods, I am not obligated to follow their example.[74] The Bible accurately and inerrantly describes these actions of the early church for our edification, but it nowhere prescribes that all churches do these things at all times.

Authority

Even within the more conservative denominations with similar doctrinal positions, there can be differences of opinion as to what the term "authority" means. Since only to the extent that Scripture is properly interpreted can it be said to be authoritative, there must be a common meaning of authority.

The New Testament uses the Greek word *exousiazo*, which is defined as to "exercise authority upon, bring under

---

[72] Matt. 4:1ff.; John 10:34.

[73] History, poetry, parable, proverb, apocalypse, Gospel, prophecy, etc.

[74] Acts 2:44-45.

the (have) power of."[75] *Vine's Complete Expository Dictionary* describes authority as "the power of one whose will and commands must be obeyed by others, as used in Matt. 28:18; John 17:2; Jude. 1:25; Rev. 12:10, 17:13."[76] *The American Dictionary of the English Language* defines authority as the "legal power, or a right to command or to act; as the authority of a prince over subject, and of parents over children."[77] Dr. Sproul writes: "The word 'authority' contains within itself the word "author." God is the author of all things which he has authority."[78] Dr. Cornelius Van Til[79] defined authority as "nothing but the placing of the absolute personality of God before the finite personality of man."[80]

Clearly, *sola Scriptura,* or the authority of Scripture over Christians, means we are to bring or give ourselves over to the control of our Creator. God has provided all of the instruction we need to live a life of obedience to His glory through His Word.

---

[75] James Strong. "The New Strong's Expanded Dictionary of the Words in the Greek New Testament." In *The New Strong's Expanded Exhaustive Concordance of the Bible.* (Nashville, TN: Thomas Nelson, 2010), reference number G1850.

[76] William Edwy Vine and Merrill F. Unger. *Vine's Complete Expository Dictionary of Old and New Testament Words for E-Sword.* EStudySource, Inc., 2006, np.

[77] Noah Webster. *American Dictionary of the English Language.* (New York: S. Converse, 1828). Reprint (Chesapeake, VA: Foundations for American Christian Education, 1995), np.

[78] R.C. Sproul. *Chosen by God.* 25th Anniversary edition. Sanford, FL: Ligonier Ministries, 1986/2011), p. 14.

[79] Early twentieth-century theologian.

[80] Cornelius Van Til. "Antitheses in Education." In *Foundations of Christian Education: Addresses to Christian Teachers*, edited by Dennis E. Johnson, 3-24. (Phillipsburg, NJ: Presbyterian and Reformed Publishing Company, 1953/1990), p. 24.

The doctrine of *sola Scriptura* is, in the end, a Christological issue. Ultimately, since our salvation is dependent on our view of who Jesus is, His view of *sola Scriptura* must be our own. The question we have to ask ourselves is this: Am I willing to hold to a different view of Scripture than one Jesus held to?

Ultimately, sola Scriptura is the foundation of the Christian curriculum framework.

Notes

SUPREMACY OF SCRIPTURE AND CURRICULUM

Now that the authority of God's Word in the life of the believer has been clearly established, how does this apply to the curriculum we expose our children to?

The first consideration in any biblical Christian curriculum development must be that of the supremacy of Scripture. Theocentric curriculum must be based upon the understanding and absolute belief that "no fact can be known unless it be known in its relationship to God."[81] The curriculum must submit to, and be aligned with, Scripture "so that the students might see in microcosm how the Scriptures are authoritative everywhere else."[82]

This can clearly be seen, for "the greatest commandment, given in the context of education, requires that we love God with all of our heart, soul, **mind**, and strength" [emphasis added].[83] Reason and emotion often squabble like tetchy siblings, but they must learn to obey their parents. Reason must submit to Scripture, and our emotions must be brought under the authority of Scripture, and it is the task of true education to see that both do so. Our body, mind,

---

[81] Louis Berkhof and Cornelius Van Til. *Foundations of Christian Education: Address to Christian Teachers.* (Dennis E. Johnson, Ed.). (Phillipsburg, NJ: Presbyterian and Reformed Publishing Co., 1990), p. 18; Randolph Crump Miller. *The Clue To Christian Education.* (New York: Scribner's Sons, 1947/1950); & C. H. Johnson. *Implications of the Method of Correlation for the Use of the Bible in Christian Education.* (Unpub doctoral diss, Columbia University, Teachers College, 1955).

[82] Douglas Wilson. *The Case For Classical Christian Education.* (Wheaton, IL: Crossway Books, 2003) p. 68; & James DeForest Murch. *Christian Education And The Local Church* (Revised). Cincinnati, OH: The Standard Publishing Company, 1958/1943).

[83] Deut. 6:4-9; Wilson, *The Case For Classical,* 2003, p. 47; Matt. 22:38 (NIV).

and spirit must be subordinated to the Word of God.[84]

Johannes Van der Walt and Gerhard Zecha, writing on how Christian teachers reflect their instruction based upon how they model what they teach, and Stephen Richard Turley writing on how an integrated or interdisciplinary curriculum provides for a more effective Christian education agree that, "if the truth of what students have to learn depended on the authority of the teacher,[85] the education program will have failed,"[86] for "it is in the inexhaustible knowledge of God from which all things emerge and in which all things cohere."[87]

After researching the effectiveness of Christian-published science textbooks in preparation for the science reasoning subtest of the American College Testing (ACT), Janice Guthrie supported this idea, acknowledging that "knowledge is based on truth, and truth is based on the character of God," and "the Holy Bible, God's written communication, is the source of truth ..."[88] Collins contends that a biblical Christian education program design must focus on the integration of theology to all other disciplines as a way to help students adapt to the "reality of Christian

---

[84] Wilson, *The Case for Classical,* 2003; & Peter M. Collins. "Thoroughly Christian and Truly a School: Developing a Christian   Secondary School," *Notre Dame Journal of Education, 5*(3) (Fall, 1974), 211-215.

[85] Parent and teacher will be used interchangeably.

[86] Johannes L. Van der Walt and Gerhard Zecha. "Philosophical-Pedagogical Criteria for Assessing the Effectiveness of a Christian School," *Journal of Research on Christian Education, 13*(2) (Fall, 2004), 167-198, p. 181.

[87] Stephen Richard Turley. "Paideia Kyriou: Biblical and Patristic Models for Intergraded Christian Curriculum." *Journal of Research on Christian Education, 18,* (2009), 125-139, p. 126; John 10:35; 2 Tim. 3:16-17.

[88] Janice Guthrie. "Christian-Published Textbooks and the Preparation of Teens for the Rigors of College Science Courses. *Journal of Research on Christian Education, 20,* (2011), 46-72, pp. 48 & 49.

understanding, belief, and living."[89]

The Purpose and Nature of Man

What one believes the nature of man to be, and what should be his purpose in life, are the guiding questions that impact all curriculum design decisions. It is impossible to construct a curriculum design program without consciously or unconsciously making a definite determination about a child's basic nature and what his purpose in life should be.[90]

In addition to a curriculum design plan being subordinate to Scripture, the content must reflect God's view of the purpose and nature of man. For the biblical Christian, it is held that the ultimate purpose of man is to glorify God and to enjoy Him forever,[91] and God has given us instruction through His Word as to how we are to glorify and enjoy Him.[92] Sin, through the fall of Adam, has corrupted every human being's nature.[93] Paul even tells us it is because of this disposition that man does not innately want to glorify God and enjoy Him forever. Instead, man is at war with God, for the fall has brought upon mankind the loss of communion with God, and as a result, we are all now born into this world as children of wrath.[94]

---

[89] Collins. "Thoroughly Christian," 1974, p. 212; Miller, *The Clue to Christian Education,* 1947/1950; Johnson, *Implications of the Method,* 1955; & Murch, *Christian Education,* 1958.

[90] John A. Stormer. *None Dare Call It Education.* (Florissant, MO: Liberty Bell Press, 1998); & Johnson, *Implications of the Method,* 1955.

[91] 1 Cor. 10:31; & Ps. 73:25-26.

[92] Eph. 2:20; 2 Tim. 3:16; & 1 John 1:3.

[93] Ps. 51:5; Job 14:4; & John 3:6.

[94] Romans 3:10, 5:16, 8:28; Gen. 3:8, 10,14; John 8:34, 42, 44; Eph. 2:12, 2:2-3; John 3:36; Rom. 1:18; & Eph. 5:6.

Modern pedagogy is based upon axiomatic humanistic thinking that man is basically good. Humanists believe people do evil because of ignorance. And if sin is ignorance, then education is salvation.[95] For example, in the humanistic faith, man does evil because he is not properly educated, and if he were taught more effectively, then the great savior — education — would straighten out all his internal kinks.[96]

On the other hand, "Christian teaching holds that man is a sinner and rebels, and he must be saved by Jesus Christ."[97] From the humanistic viewpoint, mankind is understood as *Homo sapiens*, with humans defined by their ability to think. But in the Christian's view, man is *Homo adorans*, worshiping man. "What men and women are in the presence of God defines them: in light of this, they learn to think, love, walk, emote, and sing in a certain way."[98]

Curriculum

Because of our created purpose, we must always remember, "the Christian faith is not a condiment to be

[95] Wilson, *The Case for Classical*, 2003, p. 55; Johnson, *Implications of the Method*, 1955; Michael Hogan. *Bacon and Newman: Bar God From Science.* (Jersey City, NJ: St. Peter's College Press, 1939); & Henry T. Edmondson III. *John Dewey & the Decline of an American Education.* (Wilmington, DE: ISI Books, 2006).

[96] Wilson, *The Case for Classical*, 2003, p. 45; John Dewey. *Education Today* (J. Ratner, Ed.). New York: G.P. Putnam's Sons, (1940/1897); Harold R. Rafton. "What Can We Believe?" *The Humanist, 3,* 118-124 (1953); Lloyd Morain and Mary S. Morain. *Humanism as the Next Step.* Boston: The Beacon Press (1954); Rudolf Dreikurs. "The Religion of Democracy: Part II." *The Humanist, 6,* 266-272 (1955); Johnson, *Implications of the Method*, 1955; & Murch. *Christian Education*, 1958/1943.

[97] Wilson, 2003, p. 45; Gen. 2:16,17; 3:1-6; Rom. 5:12-14; Eph. 2:1; Johnson, *Implications of the Method*, 1955; & Murch, *Christian Education*, 1958.

[98] Wilson, The Case for Classical, 2003, p. 63; James B. Jordan. (1997, October). "The Case Against Western Civilization, parts 1-7." (*Biblical Horizons Newsletter*, 1997). Accessed 26 November 2011, http://www.biblicalhorizons.com/open-book/the-case-against-western-civilization-parts-1-7; & Craig (1947) as cited in Johnson, *Implications of the Method*, 1955.

used to flavor the neutral substance of secular knowledge ..."[99] And "the mere inclusion of a course in religion or theology" does not make a curriculum design plan theocentric or even "Christian."[100] Closson puts it this way:

> [M]erely offering students a diverse view of the world ... [is not] ... a legitimate goal of Christian education. Introducing students to various perspectives in order to evaluate them in the light of revealed truth [would] ... be more appropriate.[101]

There are those who believe the teacher, not the curriculum, make an education theocentric and, therefore, believe secular curriculum can be transformed into a Christian curriculum by the individual teaching it.[102] While a case can be made for this argument, as proven in the previous chapters, the foundations of the secular curriculum have many unbelieving humanistic

---

[99] Wilson, *The Case for Classical*, 2003, p. 38.

[100] Collins. "Thoroughly Christian," 1974, p. 211.

[101] Don Closson. *Should Christians Be Studying Literature and History From Secular Textbooks?* (Plano, TX: Probe Ministries, 2008). Accessed 27 November 2011, from https://www.probe.org/should-christians-be-studying-literature-and-history-from-secular-textbooks/, n.p.; Miller, 1947; Johnson, 1955.

[102] Jody Capehart. "What Makes a Program Christian?" *Christian Early Education,* 7(11)(2000), 3-6.

practices and assumptions as its foundations.[103] If Christians imitate those practices, they will find themselves inadvertently embracing the underlying humanistic assumptions.[104] Of course, the same can be said for the vast majority of Christian publishers for they use the same pedagogy and frameworks in their curriculum design plans as their secular counterparts.

Doug Wilson warns his readers:

> If ... [Christian educators] do not ground everything ... [they] do on the teaching of Scripture, ... [their] compromise will at some point undo ... [them].[105]

With nearly 80 percent of professing evangelical Christian children turning their backs on Christ and, of these, 80 percent not coming back, and 90 percent of America's pastors refusing to teach on social issues even though they admit the Bible clearly teaches on such subjects, can we say

---

[103] Dewey, *Education Today*, 1940/1897; John Dewey. *Human Nature & Conduct.* (New York: The Modern Library, 1957/1922); Potter, *Humanism a New Religion, 1930*; Rafton, "What Can We Believe," 1953; Morain and Morain, *Humanism as the Next Step*, 1954; Dreikurs, "The Religion of Democracy," 1955; Paul C. Vitz. Censorship: *Evidence of Bias In Our Children's Textbooks.* (Ann Arbor, MI: Servant Books, 1986); William F. Pinar, William M. Reynolds, Patrick Slattery, Peter M. Taubman. *Understanding Curriculum: An Introduction To The Study of Historical and Contemporary Curriculum Discourses.* (New York: Peter Lang Publishing Inc., 1995), p. 77; Johnson, Implications of the Method, 1955, pp. 51, 52, 62; Tillich, 1950 as cited in Johnson, *Implications of the Method*, 1955; Murch, *Christian Education*, 1958/1943; & Edmondson III, *John Dewey*, 2006.

[104] Wilson, *The Case for Classical*, 2003; Collins. "Thoroughly Christian," 1974; & Edmondson III, *John Dewey*, 2006.

[105] Wilson, *The Case for Classical*, 2003, p. 133; & Murch, *Christian Education*, 1958/1943.

---

checkmate?[106] Oh and if this isn't enough to convince you how about the fact that about 10% of children from professing evangelical Christian families who attend public school hold to a biblical worldview, only 12% attending private Christian schools hold to a biblical worldview. Homeschooling has proven to fair not much better at 3% holds to biblical worldview by the time they graduate.[107]

Another aspect of a distinctively Christian philosophy of biblical education is that Christian teachers know nothing can really be known without knowing who God is.[108] In addition, Wilson writes that "... Scriptures expressly require a non-agnostic form of education."[109] The following are major distinctive elements of a biblical Christian education:

---

[106] Barna Group. (Septermber 11, 2006). "Most twentysomethings put Christianity on the shelf following spiritually active teen years." Accessed April 7, 2014 from https://www.barna.org/barna-update/article/16-teensnext-gen/147-most-twentysomethings-put-christianity-on-the-shelf-following-spiritually-active-teen-years#.U7L5Tvnxq2d; & David Kinnaman & Gabe Lyons. *unChristian: What a New Generation Really Thinks About Christianity ... And Why It Matters.* (Grand Rapids, MI: Baker Books, 2007); Chris Woodward. (01 Aug., 2014) "Barna: Many pastors wary of raising 'controversy.'" NE News Now, Retrieved September 25, 2014 from http://onenewsnow.com/church/2014/08/01/barna-many-pastors-wary-of-raising-controversy?utm_source=OneNewsNow&utm_medium=email&utm_term=167 78861&utm_content=94434134443&utm_campaign=14739#.VCSilfldW4b

[107] See episode 28 with Dan Smithwick of the Nehemiah Institute where Dan speaks on the P.E.E.R.S Worldview Assessment and what nearly 30 years of assessments and quantitative data has correlated between graduating students worldview and the worldviews they are indoctrinated in. See www.edstruggle.com/28.

[108] Berkhof and Van Til. *Foundations of Christian Education,* 1990; Turley, "Paideia Kyriou," 2009; & James W. Mohler. Youth Ministry Education and The Liberal Arts: The Need For Integration. *The Journal of Youth Ministry,* 26(2) (2004, Spring), 53-63.

[109] Douglas Wilson. *Standing On The Promise.* (Moscow, ID: Canon Press, 1997), p. 6; Craig, 1947, as cited in Johnson, *Implications of the Method,* 1955, p. 69.

1. The education of children is the responsibility of the parents and, in particular, fathers.
2. The goal of education is the salvation and discipleship of the next generation who possesses a worldview reflecting Scriptural principles.
3. Education is based on the Holy Bible as the source of absolute truth.
4. Education holds Jesus Christ as preeminent in the life of the individual.[110]

There are many who argue that the Bible is not sufficient in learning everything in the universe. Of course not and, as previously stated, it is only authoritative in areas in which it addresses. Furthermore, as Thomas Aquinas pointed out, some things are learned from nature and others are learned only by grace/revelation. While it is important to distinguish the two, we must never separate the two.

Thomas Aquinas's Diagram

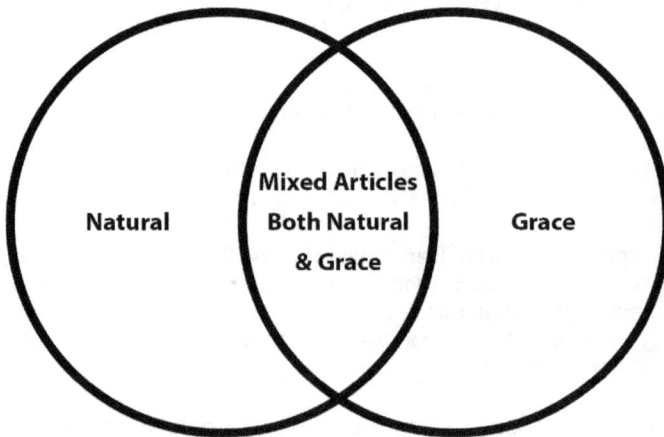

Natural

**Mixed Articles
Both Natural
& Grace**

Grace

---

[110] Guthrie. "Christian-Published Textbooks," 2011, p. 49.

What Aquinas means by these two distinctions is that there are certain truths that can only be learned in the study of nature. For example, pray as much as you want, study Scripture as hard as you would like, and you will never learn about the human digestive system or photosynthesis. He also said there are certain things that can only be learned through grace/revelation.

For example, no matter how hard or long you study the human digestive system or photosynthesis, you will never come to the understanding of Soteriology, the doctrine of salvation or the atonement of Jesus Christ, etc. So some truth can be learned from nature and some truth from revelation. Aquinas also believed truths can be found in mixed articles. These are truths that can be learned from both nature and grace. First and foremost, that God exists. Ultimately both nature and grace leads us to the same place—to God. A correct study of nature will reveal to you there is a God.[111]

Aquinas was an apostle of the unity of truth. He held that all truth meets at the top. What is true in science will ultimately confirm the truths of Scripture. In other words, truth never contradicts itself. Scientific truth may supplement Scripture, but it will not contradict Scripture. Scriptural truth will not contradict scientific truth. Science *may* correct *theology*, but never the Scriptures. You can see this play out with Galileo and the Roman Catholic Church. Galileo was correcting the church's theology, not what Scripture said, for Scripture never said the earth was the center of the universe. Theologians erroneously taught it was. It really should be the Christian that is most passionate for science for if our foundation for truth is true, then all other truth can only support and enhance it.

---

[111] Romans 1:20.

Notes

PHILOSOPHY OF
BIBLICALLY BASED EDUCATION

A biblical Christian philosophy of education comes from biblical principles and promotes a worldview that addresses truth, reality, authority, the role of the teacher, the student's responsibility, the curriculum, and pedagogy.[112] Teaching Godly living and fidelity to the Scriptures comes first, with the academics of what a student should know and be able to do, second.[113]

As Christian children are given a thoroughly and distinctively biblically Christian education, they will understand the world God placed them in, and they will understand their purpose in life in Christ and, as a result, they will embrace the terms of the covenant that define it. They will provide the kind of contrast with our postmodern culture's lost children that will make evangelism truly potent.[114]

A consistent biblical Christian pedagogy sees education as inherently religious and cannot be non-agnostic, as something that involves the whole person in the context of the whole universe, a universe created by the triune God.[115] It is important that Christian schools, as well as homeschools do not imitate in any fundamental way, the pedagogy of the

---

[112] Randolph Crump Miller. *The Clue to Christian Education*. (New York: Scribner's Sons, 1947/1950); Johnson, *Implications of the Method*, 1955; & Murch, *Christian Education*, 1958/1943.

[113] 2 Tim: 3:16; 1 Cor. 10:31; Ps 73:25-26; Guthrie, "Christian-Published Textbooks," 2011; & Murch, *Christian Education*, 1958/1943.

[114] Wilson, *The Case for Classical*, 2003.

[115] Wilson, *Standing On The Promise*, 1997; Johnson, *Implications of the Method*, 1955; & Murch, *Christian Education*, 1958/1943.

government school system.[116]

Christian textbooks alone are not enough to ensure a child receives an authentic Christian education for:

> [C]omfort is not found in Christian-published texts themselves but in their use as tools to reinforce what is done and said by the teacher in and outside of the classroom. Likewise, Christian school teachers using secular-published textbooks need to be vigilant in seeking opportunities to exegete scripture and interpret the theories and applications of science within the contours of a biblical worldview.[117]

The difference between Christian and secular content in Christian textbooks may be similar to content found in state and national standards, but the basic assumptions under which it is taught are uniquely different.

For example, the structured, systematic hierarchy of knowledge points to God, and unified subject content under the umbrella of the creation-fall-redemption theme will not be present in state or national standards, but are essential to a biblical Christian education; in fact **without it, you simply do not have any measure of a biblical Christian education**.[118]

---

[116] Wilson, *The Case for Classical*, 2003; Johannes L. Van der Walt and Gerhard Zecha. "Philosophical-Pedagogical Criteria for Assessing the Effectiveness of a Christian School," *Journal of Research on Christian Education*, 13(2) (Fall, 2004), 167-198; & Collins, "Thoroughly Christian," 1974; Potter, *Humanism a New Religion, 1930*; & Murch, *Christian Education*, 1958/1943.

[117] Guthrie, "Christian-Published Textbooks," 2011, p. 68; Wilson, The Case for Classical, 2003, p. 19, 38, 133; Robert L. Jackson. "Retooling Education: Testing and The Liberal Arts." *Acad. Quest*, 20, 332-346 (December 2007), p. 342; Collins, "Thoroughly Christian," 1974, p. 214; & Vitz, *Censorship*, 1986.

[118] Guthrie, "Christian-Published Textbooks," 2011; Vitz, *Censorship*, 1986; Pinar, *at el*, *Understanding Curriculum*, 1995; & Johnson, *Implications of the Method*, 1955.

Biblically based Christians want their children to live out their Christian lifestyle and worldview which requires integration of faith, life, and learning.[119]

> Jesus Christ is the *arche*, the one in whom all things hold together (Col. 1:18). But Christ is not a mere word we use: Jesus Christ is the Son of God, seated at the right hand of God the Father. There is no Christian worldview where He is not present ... Education that does not begin and end in heaven is not true education.[120]

As you can see, the curriculum your children are exposed to matters, for curriculum is:

> [T]he vehicle that facilitates the personal transformation of the student toward a mature relationship with Jesus Christ, enabling the student to separate truth from error in all aspects of life.[121]

[119] Mohler, *Youth Ministry Education*, 2004; Collins, "Thoroughly Christian," 1974; & Johnson, *Implications of the Method*, 1955.

[120] Wilson, *The Case for Classical, 2003*, p. 65.

[121] Guthrie, "Christian-Published Textbooks," 2011, p. 49; & Johnson, *Implications of the Method*, 1955.

SECTION 3

PLAN OF ACTION

BIBLICAL CHRISTIAN CURRICULUM DEVELOPMENT: CONCEPTUAL FRAMEWORK

Ok, so up to this point we have examined the six prevailing worldviews, existentialism, humanism, pragmatism, positivism, pluralism, and hedonism, which has lead us to a post-Christian society. In section two, we examined what it means to have a Christian curriculum framework beginning with the inerrancy and authority of Scripture in all areas in which Scriptures addresses, and the philosophy of biblically based education. We concluded section two with an example of a conceptional biblical Christian curriculum design plan parents could use right away.

In this final section, we are going to provide you an plan of action. We are going to move from the conceptual to the practical hands-on in terms of what to teach. We'll begin with the methodology, and suggested subjects for both lower and upper grades. By the end of this section, you should be equipped to provide a biblical Christian framework in your homeschool, private school, or homeschool co-op

Robert Jackson reports:

> The surfeit of ideas on curriculum indicates a near desperation to find the next, new thing. And yet, in spite of multitudes of theories, we are surrounded by the odor of educational decay — failing schools, substandard national test scores in international comparisons, functional illiteracy among graduates ...[122]

---

[122] Jackson, "Retooling Education," 2007, p. 339; & Jordan, *The Case Against Western Civilization*, 1997.

Edie Goldenberg provides an antidote to this decay:

> More than ever before, a liberal arts education is of special value today. A successful liberal arts experience can be a source of personal satisfaction for students throughout their lives. It has staying power beyond the short half-life of technical training because it introduces students to fundamental issues as they have been explored by others through the ages.[123]

It is important to understand that, when a state takes over the responsibilities for education from parents (in particular Christian parents), the state does not disown all religions but disestablished Christianity in favor of its own statist religion in the form of humanism.

Most people, including Christians, believe religion and theology can be kept separate from education, but this simply is not true. At one time, Columbia Teachers College openly admitted religion was the framework of education.

> Religion as ultimate concern therefore provides the large framework within which education occurs ... Religious concern (whether or not recognized and designated as such) is the motive which actuates the educator and produces the general pattern of his work ... A significant test of the governing religious convictions of a person or group is the character of the education promoted by that person or group.[124]

---

[123] Eddie N. Goldenberg. "Teaching Key Competencies in Liberal Arts Education." *New Directions for Teaching and Learning*, 85, 15-23, (2001, Spring), p. 16.

[124] Philip H. Phenix. *Religious Concerns In Contemporary Education.* (Bureau of Publications, Teachers College, Columbia University, 1959), p. 19.

Not only does education find its foundation in religion, but educational standards express the religious standards and expectations of a culture.

The English word "curriculum" is taken directly from the Latin in meaning and spelling. Curriculum, correctly defined, means "running, a race, chariot," and is cognate with the Latin verb, *currere*, "to run." A curriculum is therefore the chariot, race course, or vehicle whereby a culture expresses its religious faith and standards.

While nearly all research into curriculum design frameworks is based upon humanistic assumptions, selective frameworks will lend itself to a biblical Christian curriculum if adapted to scripturally aligned foundations. For example, Miller and Seller's three metaorientations of transmission, transaction, and transformation positions can work in theory for a biblical Christian curriculum framework, but their fundamental assumptions are clearly incompatible with Scripture, for Miller and Seller state the assumptions that support their definition and paradigm has a "humanistic orientation."[125] The same issue arises with Nikitina's contextualizing, conceptualizing, and problem-centering metaorientations.[126]

While Miller and Seller's, and Nikitina's assumptions and presuppositions, are incompatible with a biblical Christian worldview, they use the same framework as Adler's,

[125] John P. Miller & Wayne Seller. *Curriculum Perspectives and Practice.* (Toronto: Copp Clark Pitman Ltd., 1990), p. 147.

[126] Svetlana Nikitina. "Three Strategies For Interdisciplinary Teaching: Contextualizing, Conceptualizing, and Problem-Centering. *Journal of Curriculum Studies, 38*(3) (2006), 251-271.

Roberts' and Billings' Didactic, Coaching, and Seminar,[127] and the metaorientations described as grammar, logic, and rhetoric by Wilson, Veith & Kern, Hart, Rickover; and Kern's tradition/content, truth/ideas, and virtues/skills—all of which are complementary.[128] These frameworks can be summed up as the *trivium* and *quadrivium* used with the traditional seven liberal arts, the same education design recommended by the Committee of Ten and has proven itself over the past two thousand years.

The basic curriculum is called the liberal arts curriculum ("liberal" from the Latin *liber* [free] and it is a course in the arts of freedom, or a vehicle in the arts of liberty).

The origin of the modern liberal arts curriculum is in Greek humanism—in the original and classical sense. In other words, it was a process of educating man in his true form: the real and genuine human nature. It was through a liberal arts curriculum that the Hellenist answered the question, what is liberty? And, how does a man prepare himself to be a free man?

The Greek liberal arts are a man-centered and anti-Christian answer to the question. "How shall a man be free?" Another way to ask this: "How shall a man be saved?" The liberal arts curriculum is thus the vehicle of liberty and

---

[127] Terry Roberts & Laura Billings *The Paideia Classroom: Teaching for Understanding.* (Larchmont: NY: Eye on Education, 1999); Mortimer J. Adler. *The Paideia Proposal: An Educational Manifesto.* (New York: Touchstone, 1998); & Jackson, "Retooling Education," 2007.

[128] Wilson, *Standing On The Promise*, 1997; Wilson, The Case for Classical, 2003, Gene Edward Veith & Andrew Kern. Classical Education: The Movement Sweeping America. (Washington, D.C.: Capital Research Center, 2001); Randall D. Hart. *Increasing Academic Achievement With The Trivium of Classical Education.* (Lincoln, NE: IUniverse, 2006); Rickover,1962 as cited in Peter F. Oliva. *Developing The Curriculum,* (3rd ed.). (New York: HarperCollins Publishers, 1992); & Andrew Kern. "On Curriculum Development." (*The Circe Institute, August 23, 2011).* Accessed 23 August 2011, from http://circeinstitute.com/2011/08/on-curriculum-development.

salvation. It is the way a culture, a people, saves its children from evil and prepares them for life with the skills, knowledge, and abilities required to be and remain free. This is inescapably a religious task. A historical note: the apostle Paul was classically educated and was thought to be the most educated man alive at the time. I am not suggesting the pagan Greek classical school is what Christians should offer, but it is the pedagogy, content, and desire for truth, goodness, and beauty they were searching for. After all, we should be seeking the same for all truth is God's truth. As we can see Paul with his classical Greek and **Jewish** education, he was intellectually prepared to fulfill his calling when Christ called him to do the work he was destined to do.

Greek education was structuring for the *polis*, the city state. The eighth century saw the birth of the Greek *polis*. A *polis* was a community with its separate political organization. The word "political" is derived from *polis*. This term is translated as city-state. Often the *polis* formed due to the geography of the region such as mountain ranges and seas creating natural barriers from other tribes and regions forcing the area to form a separate governance and culture. Athens and Sparta are two famous Greek *polies*. The Greeks regarded life in a *polis* as the most ideal and most humane form of existence.[129]

According to Aristotle, man was a political animal and was to be educated into the life-saving state. Plato's *Republic* laid out a total education design plan for total statism. Statism can be defined as the belief that concentration of economic controls and planning should be in the hands of a highly centralized government often extending to government ownership of industry. Often this is associated with socialism

---

[129] L. De Blois and R.J. Van Der Spek. *An Introduction to the Ancient World.* (London: Routledge, 1997.), pgs. 72-73)

and communism.[130] Statist believes in the supremacy of the government and often used what French historian Alexis de Tocqueville described as soft tyranny. Soft tyranny eventually becomes increasingly more oppressive, leading to a hard tyranny, or as we call it today, totalitarianism.[131]

This was clearly emphasized by the Romans, for their educational aim was "the subordination of the individual to the city."[132] Man's salvation, his liberty, was to be found in the City of Man. After all, from the Greek and Roman worldview, the chief end of man was to glorify the state and to serve and enjoy it all of his short life.

A Christian order did emerge, however. The Reformation emphasized the sovereignty of God and the total scope of His law. The purpose of education and curriculum was to prepare man to glorify God, to enjoy Him, and to serve Him through God's ordained calling. However, the prevalence of Platonistic and neo-Platonistic strains of humanism during the Renaissance undermined theocentric emphasis of the Reformation. Instead of emphasizing the state as the "true *polis*," as Plato did in *The Republic*, the Renaissance emphasized the amoral power-state and for the individual, anarchistic man. This meant that the state equaled tyranny and, for the individual, anarchy. This is not a coincidence. Both are products of nihilism, relativism, and pragmatism.

Hitler's Germany, Stalin's Russia, Moa's China, Asaid's Seria, and Castro's Cuba are the best examples of this. All of these governments were, and some remain tyrannical. The sole purpose of the individual existence is to serve the State.

---

[130] "Statism." *Merriam-Webster.Com*. Accessed January 13, 2015 from www.merriam-webster.com/dictionary/statism.

[131] Alexis de Tocqueville. *Democracy in America*. (New York: Penguin, 2003).

[132] Pierre Grimal. *The Civilization of Rome*. W.S. Maguinnes, Trans. (NY: Simon and Schuster, 1963), p. 100.

Your desires have no relevance and in fact, if you allowed yourself to have personal desires that were not aligned with the States you would be considered selfish in places like Moa's China. None of these governments believed there was a time before or a time after your lived, nothing before your existence. Your only reason to live is ultimately based upon the benefit you bring to the State. It's easy to see how an individual can move towards individualized anarchy for if you are nothing but fodder for the state, then what is the point of civilized life? Why not try to get what you can get where ever and by any means for you live today, and tomorrow you may die?

On the other hand, when God is man's universal, his source of life, man becomes dependent upon God, and God becomes the focus of man's life. God becomes the source of law, the standard of truth, and our only hope of salvation. With God as his center, man carries out his calling in *corum deo,* in the presence of God. When you live in *corum deo,* you are independent of the state because God becomes your ultimate authority and source of all things. For the humanist, however, man has become his own god. Instead of depending on God, he depends on the state, and instead of living for God, he lives for the approval of man.

In every man-centered faith, "the individual needs society as a resonance box."[133] For humanism, man is his own law and his own lawmaker, as a result, social approval becomes the best test of law. This standard leads to the socialization of life, law, and living instead of declaring God as the universal, and the course of meaning and being. Therefore, wherever education becomes humanistic, it will produce both statism and anarchistic individuals. Furthermore, a curriculum which professes to be Christian because it includes religious instruction, but is in all other

---

[133] John Simon White. *Renaissance Cavalier.* (NY: Philosophical Library, 1959), p. 7.

ways humanistic in orientation, will also breed statism and anarchism.

After the Reformation, the Enlightenment came as a counter-movement resulting in a revival of ancient Greco-Roman humanism. Its philosophical premise was the dialectic, or discussion and reasoning, of nature and liberty. Nature became the substitute concept for God, and natural law took the place of the transcendent written word of God. But after Darwin, nature was removed as a source of law due to Evolution's description of nature as blindly evolving randomly without mind or reason. With nature removed as a source of law, man's law was all that remained if there was to be any law at all. As a result, statism succeeded the older liberalism of natural law and became the ultimate source of authority and law for those who came after the Enlightenment.

With man as the ultimate authority, this new law is really anti-law for in their denial of any absolute law in the universe and, thus, an absolute lawgiver, any truth must be pragmatic truth. As a result, the whole curriculum becomes progressive (i.e., instrumental). No subject embodies any truth; all ideas are tools for man's use in self-realization. From the humanist worldview, liberty means freedom from law as absolute, law as embodying truth and moral order.

So why is this important? As stated in previous chapters, this is important because, from this viewpoint, all ideas are equally valid and equally false. The measure of each idea is based upon their utility, instrumentality, and nothing more. For curriculum, this means teaching children relativism instead of absolute subject matter. This means teaching children that no truth exists except man and the realization of himself through the Great Society of Dewey and company.

For Dewey, Christianity with its belief in right and wrong, good and evil, heaven and hell, the saved and the lost, was anti-democratic and irreconcilable with a democratic society.[134] For Dewey, biblical Christianity had no place in the curriculum and in his Great Society. In this view, to hold democracy and equality and maintain a family-based society that is aristocratic, creates "a perpetual compromise" that ensures that "inequality of opportunity is automatically, and often unconsciously, a basic principle of the nation."[135]

With all of this said, a biblical Christian liberal arts education is the best preparation either for postsecondary education or entering the job market.[136] Roberts and Billings' stresses a rigorous academic program for all children in the context of a whole-school program of reform. The liberal arts "are not simply 'compatible' or even 'complementary' for tomorrow. They are 'transformational' and help to transform one's character and worldview into a godly one. But this requires consistency in teaching philosophies across disciplines."[137]

Kern's paradigm is ideal for the biblical Christian.[138] This framework is naturally subordinate to Scripture and provides a design that will give the best opportunity for students to have the intellect needed in order to successfully fulfill their God-ordained purpose in life. Shall we examine how these frameworks work together?

---

[134] John Dewey. *A common Faith.* (NY: Yale University Press, 1934), p. 84.

[135] James Bryant Conant. *Education In A Divided World, The Function of the Public Schools In Our Unique Society.* (Cambridge: Harvard University Press, 1948), p. 8.

[136] Roberts & Billings, *The Paideia Classroom*, 1999.

[137] Mohler, *Youth Ministry Education*, 2004, p. 58.

[138] Murch, *Christian Education*, 1958/1943.

Emphasis of the Trivium

GRAMMAR STAGE Grades K-5	LOGIC STAGE Grades 6-8	RHETORIC STAGE Grades 9-12
Grammar	Grammar	Grammar
	Logic	Logic
Logic		Rhetoric
Rhetoric	Rhetoric	

Tradition/Content/Didactic/Grammar/Transmission/Contextualizing

Elementary curriculum needs to focus on didactic instruction of factual information and the "accumulation of factoids"[139] or, as Adler describes it, "acquisition of knowledge"[140] "through texts, lectures, demonstrations, and a wide range of audiovisual material."[141] Nikitina would describe this as embedding ... disciplinary material in the fabric of time, culture, and personal experience" which "is the prototypical mode for generating knowledge ..."[142]

The goal of didactic instruction is to provide students with a body of information they can apply and manipulate in the next two orientations.[143]

---

[139] Wilson, *The Case for Classical*, 2003, p. 132; Hart, *Increasing Academic Achievement*, 2006; Veith & Kern, *Classical Education*, 2001; & Kern, "On Curriculum Development," 2011.

[140] Adler, *The Paideia Proposal*, 1998, p. 22.

[141] Roberts & Billings, *The Paideia Classroom*, 1999, p. 9.

[142] Nikitina. "Three strategies," 2006, pp. 252, 256-57.

[143] Roberts & Billings, *The Paideia Classroom*, 1999.

*Truth/Ideas/Coaching/Dialectic (Logic)/Transaction/ Concept-
ualizing*

Curriculum for what would be considered today as middle school should be focused on *truth/ideas* or, as Adler refers to it, "development of skill"[144] and, as Roberts and Billings[145] calls it, "coaching intellectual skills." Wilson describes this orientation as the "sorting out of facts into truth and goodness."[146] In this orientation, students are coached to evaluate knowledge, think critically about it, solve problems with it, and consciously develop a biblical Christian worldview.[147]

In doing so, *truth/ideas* "involves identifying core concepts that are central to two or more disciplines ... and establishing a rigorous quantifiable connection among them."[148] This integrative strategy is designed to takescientific and mathematical thinking beyond the facts and singular theories to the level of the underlying concepts. Such core concepts as linearity, change, and scale can effectively tie together algebra and geometry, physics and biology, history and geography, history and civics, illuminating hidden pattern of relationships. The goal of this mode of integration is not to interpret human experience, but to understand essential laws of the world that operate regardless of our perception and interpretation.[149]

---

[144] Adler, *The Paideia Proposal*, 1998, p. 25.

[145] Roberts & Billings, *The Paideia Classroom*, 1999, p. 6.

[146] Wilson, *The Case for Classical*, 2003, pp. 132-133; & Veith & Kern, *Classical Education*, 2001.

[147] Van der Walt and Zecha, "Philosophical-Pedagogical Criteria," 2004.

[148] Nikitina. "Three strategies," 2006, p. 253.

[149] Nikitina. "Three strategies," 2006.

Academic coaching should result in a product-oriented project that becomes the organizing principle for all three metaorientations.[150] The goal of the coached project is to "put students in the position of having to manipulate and apply that knowledge in a context that is relevant to them personally."[151]

Virtue/Skills/Seminar/Rhetoric/Transformation/Problem-Solving

Upper school curriculum design utilizes the *virtue/skills* orientation by "enlarging students' understanding."[152] Students do this by discussing values and ideas through seminar discussions, adaptive use, and synthesis of various rhetorical devices (fable, comparison, figure, etc.). In turn, students will be able to experience mastery as they use language—in writing and in speech—to convey knowledge, passion, and craftsmanship.[153]

Van der Walt and Zecha writes that, during this orientation, teachers should gradually and consistently diminish their own organizing and direction, and encourage students to take charge and be more self-directed.[154] Nikitina agrees that this orientation involves enlisting the knowledge and modes of thinking in several disciplines in order to examine real-life problems.[155] In a more abstract form, Roberts and Billings and Wilson argue that the goal of this orientation "is to have them learn to think abstractly and

---

[150] Roberts & Billings, *The Paideia Classroom*, 1999.

[151] Roberts & Billings, *The Paideia Classroom*, 1999, p. 10.

[152] Adler, *The Paideia Proposal*, 1998, p. 28.

[153] Roberts & Billings, *The Paideia Classroom*, 1999; & Jackson, "Retooling Education," 2007.

[154] Van der Walt and Zecha, "Philosophical-Pedagogical Criteria," 2004.

[155] Nikitina. "Three strategies," 2006.

communicate clearly about ideas of truth and goodness in a lovely form"[156] so that they develop the ability to:

1. Discuss and understand ideas and values
2. Solve abstract problems
3. Make more mature and more sophisticated decisions
4. Resolve conflicts between people and ideas[157]

In addition to academic coaching, parents/teachers also model to their students a Christ-like lifestyle so "both parents/teacher and student reciprocally grow together in Christlikeness."[158] Biblically based Christian educators see education as connected with the whole life, and that education has "to be a *paideia Christi.*"[159]

This cumulating orientation finishes with graduating students "not merely doing the right things, but enjoying the right things—not merely industrious, but to love industry—not merely learned, but to love knowledge—not merely pure, but to love purity—not merely just, but to hunger and thirst after justice" and a thirst for what is truly good, beautiful, and truthful based upon God's character and nature.[160]

Kern believes the place to begin when designing a curriculum plan is with *the truth/ideas* of the content because thinking is done with and about ideas, and its goal is to discover and perceive truth. Kern goes on to suggest

---

[156] Roberts & Billings, *The Paideia Classroom*, 1999, p. 11; Wilson, *The Case for Classical,* 2003, pp. 132-133; Veith & Kern, *Classical Education*, 2001.

[157] Roberts & Billings, *The Paideia Classroom*, 1999, p. 41.

[158] Turley, "Paideia Kyriou," 2009, p. 137.

[159] Van der Walt and Zecha, "Philosophical-Pedagogical Criteria," 2004, p. 183; Miller. *The Clue to Christian Education*, 1947/1950; Johnson, *Implications of the Method,* 1955.

[160] John Ruskin. *The Works of John Ruskin* (E. T. Cook & A. Wedderburn, Eds.). (New York: Longmans Green, 1905), pp. 435-436; Johnson, *Implications of the Method*, 1955; & Murch, *Christian Education*, 1958/1943.

approaching truth and ideas from the following three levels:

1. The transcendent ideas that should permeate all instruction regardless of age, class, or circumstance. For example, students should be studying or perceiving truth, goodness, beauty, freedom, justice, equity, being, mode, change, glory, honor, immortality, wisdom, virtue, and community. They always are anyway, so we might as well do it on purpose.

2. The core ideas in a domain of knowledge, from K-12. For example, leadership transitions are a constant problem of every human community, from families to schools, to states, to empires. Students will study this by necessity if they study an honest history class. So leadership transitions are a core idea in history. In literature, a core idea would be imitation. In science, modes of being and causes of change. And so on.

3. The core ideas in a domain of knowledge during a certain stage of learning. For example, elementary school children need to be studying Roman history. The parent/teacher should ask, "What truths/ideas do I want my student to contemplate this year?" Scan the 15 ideas above (level 1) and scan Roman history and ask which might be particularly fruitful. Then find stories that embody them. Justice is, of course, the ubiquitous historical question and can be explored rather easily by asking whether people should have done things: Should Brutus have assassinated Tarquinius Superbus?, Should Cincinattus have gone back to his farm?, etc.[161] Furthermore, it should be asked, what does Scripture have to say about the subject, topic, or actions, etc?

---

[161] Kern, "On Curriculum Development," 2011, pp. 1-2; Oliva, *Developing The Curriculum*, 1992.

Notes

PEDAGOGY FOR A FREEMAN

As previously stated, the educational system, or framework, called "classical education," or liberal arts, was developed over two millennia with the goal of developing young minds to be wise and free. We could define classical in a general philosophical way as "how to think and what to do." It is not pragmatism for it does not train children so they can get a "good job" — vocationalism. It is not progressivism for it is not political indoctrination — what to think. It does begin with the end in mind, and that end is to bring the child up in the love and admiration of the Lord and as a byproduct saving western civilization by passing on a Biblical Christian culture and heritage.

The foundation of today's Christian and classical education is the *trivium* and the *quadrivium*, both developed in the Middle Ages. The *trivium's* three phases of learning are adapted to three faces of development in students — grammar, logic, and rhetoric. The *quadrivium* represents four kinds of learning made of the study of mathematics, music, astronomy, and geometry.[162]

Definitions:

- *Grammar:* The fundamental rules and data of each subject.
- *Logic:* The ordered relationship of particulars in each subject.
- *Rhetoric:* The means by which the grammar and logic of each subject may be expressed clearly.

As it is used here, the word "classical" refers to the structure and form of the education provided. It also refers to the content of the studies.

---

[162] Kern, "On Curriculum Development," 2011.

In all its levels, programs, and teaching, the classical teacher seeks to do the following:

1. Emphasize grammar, logic, and rhetoric in all subjects. The structure of curriculum is traditional with a strong emphasis on the "basics."

    The "basics" include subjects such as mathematics, history, and language studies. Not only are these subjects covered, they are covered in a particular way. For example, in science, students will not only read their text, they will also read from primary sources.[163]

    Grammar, logic, and rhetoric will be emphasized in all subjects. By grammar, we mean the fundamental rules of <u>each subject</u> (we do not limit grammar to language studies). In English, a singular noun does not take a plural verb. In logic, *A* does not equal *A*. In history, time is linear, not cyclic. Each subject has its own grammar which the students need to learn. This enables the student to learn the subject from the inside out.

    The logic of each subject refers to the ordered relationship of that subject's particulars. What is the relationship between the Reformation and the colonization of America? What is the relationship between the subject and object of a sentence? As students learn the underlying rules or principles of a subject (grammar), along with how the particulars of that subject relate to each other (logic), they are learning to *think*. They are not simply memorizing fragmented pieces of knowledge.

---

[163] e.g. *How a Pump Lifts Water* by Galileo Galilei, or *The Nature of Heat* by Benjamin Franklin.

The last emphasis is rhetoric. As Christian parents, we want our children to be able to express clearly everything they learn. An essay in history must be written as clearly as if it were an English paper. An oral presentation in science should be as coherent as possible. It is not enough that the "history" or "science" is correct. This must also be expressed well.

2. Encourage every student to develop a love for learning and live up to his intellectual potential.

This goal is impossible to realize unless the *parents* have a real love for the subject. If the teacher is not excited about having this knowledge, then why should the student be excited about acquiring it? Necessity may induce the student to learn the material; it will not induce him to love it. If he does not love it, he will content himself with some minimum standard. The origin of this travesty of education is a teacher who also is content with some minimum standard. A parent or teacher who is excited about the subject he teaches will be extremely sensitive to those students who are seemingly bored.

If this goal is successfully reached, then the student will spend the rest of his life building on the foundation laid during his primary and secondary years. Not only did he receive the tools of learning, he acquired the desire to use them. Unlike most tools, they do not wear out with use.

3. Provide an orderly atmosphere conducive to the attainment of the above goals.

There is only one way to maintain an orderly atmosphere, and that is by means of firm, loving discipline. It is possible for discipline to be strict without ceasing to be fair or loving. Indeed, when discipline lapses, fairness and love are usually the first casualties. There is no way to love or instruct a child in the midst of chaos.

The Trivium

Grammar Stage of Development: Children (grades K-6) are uniquely adapted to memorize. They learn chants, songs, and rhythmic verses well and can be taught an enormous amount of information, much of which is retained for a lifetime. Students exercising this ability remain practiced in the art of memorizing.

Progressive educators often overlook memorizing once the student learns to read and write in about the third grade. As with any skills, if you do not develop memory at this phase, you will lose it. Students so enjoy memorizing that they will make up playground songs or chants of their own.[164]This is the same as educational current practices with one exception. The difference is in the attitude of the teachers. Teachers must not treat these activities as "subjects" in themselves but instead focus on gathering material for use in the next part of the *trivium.* These teachers understand that their students must absorb all the information, so they are able to be successful in the logic stage of the *trivium.* If times tables are not known, their computations will be greatly hindered if not outright impossible later on.

Logic Stage of Development: Early adolescent children (grades 6-8) become argumentative. Their ability to draw conclusions from a series of facts begins to develop. This is called the dialectic, or logic, phase. Most progressive educators overlook

---

[164] Kern, "On Curriculum Development," 2011.

this phase, except with regard to higher math. From a classical and Christian framework, teaching formal logic, logical fallacies, and reasoning skills through tools like the Socratic Method and Aristotelian logic is crucial. In this phase, the subject matter is not as important as the ends the students are able to draw from the knowledge.[165]

Rhetoric Stage of Development: In high school, students begin to develop a sense of how others perceive them. They become self-conscious about fashion, vocabulary, mannerisms, and various other forms of expression. Classicists call this the rhetoric phase. Students in this phase learn to speak and write well. They learn to relate to their audience with clarity and persuasion. Without the ability to communicate, the best ideas go unheard and are impotent.[166]

Classical education places an emphasis on the following:

- The use of classical books and art
- A general preference for great art, music, and literature of the Western Canon
- An integrated curriculum
- Idea-focused teaching
- Strong instruction in history
- The Seven Liberal Arts
  - The three arts of the *Trivium* consist of:
    - Grammar
      - The fundamental rules of each subject
    - Logic/Dialectics
      - The ordered relationship of particulars in each subject
    - Rhetoric

---

[165] Veith & Kern, *Classical Education*, 2001.

[166] *Ibid.*

- How grammar and logic of each subject may be clearly expressed
  o The four arts of the *Quadrivium* consist of:
    - Arithmetic
    - Geometry
    - Music
    - Astronomy

1. Classical education treats classical languages and mathematics as the organizing principles of education. These subjects can only be mastered by orderly, systematic study over a period of many years. They provide the best training for "learning how to learn" and the most solid foundation for further study in literature, history, and science.

2. Classical and Christian education recognizes that memory, analysis, and expression are important facets of learning at all levels. It, therefore, treats the medieval *trivium* subjects—Latin,[167] grammar, logic, and rhetoric—as disciplines in their own right. It suggests that to place undue emphasis on "ages and stages" can lead to rigidity in the curriculum and an unnatural emphasis on technique in teaching.

3. Classical and Christian education is holistic. It trains not only the mind, but also the emotions, the will, and the aesthetic sense. It fosters love for the Good, the True, and the Beautiful based upon the character and nature of God wherever they may be found. Its goal is to produce men and women both knowledgeable and virtuous.

---

[167] Reason for Latin will be discussed later.

Classical and Christian education is traditional and conservative in the sense that it seeks to pass on to each new generation "the best that has been thought and said in the world." It stands for the Permanent Things. It militates against chronological snobbery by setting our current concerns against the backdrop of history and requiring us to take long views. It lays upon us the responsibility of doing our part to preserve and transmit the accumulated wisdom of the human race.

4. Classical and Christian education rests on the principle of *multum non multa*: quality, not quantity. It does not let the good crowd out the best. Rather than rushing students from book to book, from author to author, classical and Christian education invites students to contemplate the representative masterpieces of each historical period. It gives entree into the Great Conversation by allowing students to speak at length with the master teachers of the last three millennia.[168]

When you look at the giants of the Christian faith, read their writings, you will quickly see how converse they were in the great literature of the world. But you might say, doesn't the Bible say, "Beware of vainfull philosophy"? But then how in the world can you be aware of something unless you have become aware of it? "I do not ask you to take them out of the world but that you keep them from evil" This is no doubt a fine

---

[168] In regards to literature, the Western Canon is a term to denote a canon of books, and, more widely, music, and art, that has been the most influential and enduring in demonstrating what is true, what if good, and what is beautiful across time. We read the works of the greatest writers of our western tradition, to understand what these writers have thought, felt, and imagined. And having shared their thoughts, students will know where ideas by which they live come from, and will understand better something of their position in time and space. For the Christian, these ideas must be examined against the Word of God and thus the student will be able to see the holistic creation-fall-redemption plan of God.

line to walk. The world is a threatening place for someone to make a spiritual pilgrimage. But it is the only place we can have a pilgrimage, and it happens to be the arena of redemption.

5. Classical and Christian education unites the great cultural and intellectual streams of the West, rising from Jerusalem, Athens, and Rome. As such, it represents the common cultural patrimony of all beliefs.

Instructional Methods

As a foundation, there are three things we learn, and we learn them in three ways. All three ways of how we learn apply in varying degrees to each of the three kinds of things we learn.

1. Three things we learn:
    i. Knowledge of content
    ii. Understanding/appreciation of ideas
    iii. Mastery of skills
2. Three ways we learn:
    i. Inductive
        1. Experience
    ii. Deductive
        1. Reason
    iii. By authority
        1. Subject Matter Experts

When we learn inductively, we begin with particular experiences, and then the mind goes to work comparing them. As it does so, it is identifying common features and unique features of the individual experiences and drawing conclusions (abstracting ideas) from them. Thus, we learn what red is when we are very little by seeing multiple objects that have red in them, and we learn to differentiate redness from other colors. At some point we hear the name "red" applied to those red things, so we call them red. This is also how we learn and understand the meaning of justice, freedom, beauty, etc. This is best described as learning through examples or models. The implications are extensive.

When we learn deductively, we begin with an idea (that we have already learned something about inductively) and draw logical implications. This is the learning taught by Euclid's Geometry, for example. If justice is treating things as they ought to be treated, then I cannot treat a child like a stimulus/response mechanism. Note first the principle, then the deduction or application. Socratic instruction equips people to learn this way.

When we learn by authority, we learn through the experiences and reasoning of others. I learn that Washington crossed the Delaware because historians (authorities on history) tell me so. I learn that Shakespeare wrote Hamlet because authorities tell me so. I learn that it is wrong to lie because authorities tell me so (and my conscience agrees). This is the strength of the classical program, and it is also the foundation for the idea of western "tradition."

Each mode of learning matures with the age of the child. In teaching, the goal is to arouse and train the faculties of a child's perception—the senses, the intellect, and the soul. Thus, learning best occurs in an environment that embodies the ideas to be taught, through people who authoritatively embody the ideas to be taught in their actions, words, and productions, in a prudently blended mixture of modeling, lecturing, discussing, and discovering. This is accomplished through the *trivium* and *quadrivium*.

Rooting our instruction methods in this idea, all students will be capable of fulfilling their individual potential. The following are more detailed applications of the *trivium* instructional methods.

a. The *Dialectic Method (Socratic Method)* encourages learning through the sharing of information and concepts within a group, with the thinking process playing an important role. A teacher would think of it as the relentless pursuit of truth through unceasing questions. To engage in this method, the teacher would establish their goal to clearly understand truth and move on. Once he has grown comfortable with questioning his students, they will refine his dialectic instruction. This form of questioning falls into two stages: the ironic, and the maieutic.

In the ironic stage, the teacher uses questions to probe student's understanding to find the inadequacies in the student's thoughts. These inadequacies might include contradictions, insufficient definitions of terms, faulty logic (especially things like hasty generalizations and reversal of cause and effect), and other common mistakes that people make all too frequently. The purpose of the ironic stage is to weaken the individual's confidence in an inadequate understanding of reality.

After the student recognizes the inadequacy of his original idea and wants a clearer apprehension of the truth, he is ready for the maieutic stage. In this second stage, the teacher will make more suggestions than he did in the ironic stage, but questions still drive the student. In the end, the student and the teacher both better understand the idea. The purpose of the maieutic stage is to give birth ("maieutic" is Greek for "having to do with a midwife") to this more accurate understanding of reality.

It is important to notice that both the didactic and dialectic methods of teaching are engaged in thinking about ideas by asking questions. There is no more effective method for training the mind.[169]

---

[169] Kern, "On Curriculum Development," 2011.

b. The *Didactic Method* presents models to the students for mutual contemplation. For example, if a teacher wants her students to understand Renaissance art, then she will set some Renaissance works of art in front of both the class and herself, and they will contemplate them together. If the teacher wants her students to learn a proof in geometry, she will set some examples of that proof before them and examine them together. If the teacher wants her students to know a poetic device, a noble soul, or a musical idea, she will place before the class examples of the poetic device, the noble soul, or the musical idea.

In this approach, to didactic instruction, the teacher and the student are engaged in a mutual contemplation. Both are actively thinking about the models placed before them and, as a result, both move toward a more accurate understanding of the ideas contained in the object.

Didactic instruction begins with an idea a teacher wants students to understand. Then she will find examples of the idea and, together, analyze each model individually for its properties and qualities. She will then compare the models with each other to find common features. Finally, she will compare the models with other models of different types. This enables the teacher and the students to establish what is unique to the idea they are contemplating.

This method is very effective when the teacher wants her students to understand an idea or interpret an artifact (e.g. a painting, musical composition, text, etc.). Teachers can use it effectively in science, art, music, math, and languages. It is also a wonderful way to approach children's reading.[170]

---

[170] Kern, "On Curriculum Development," 2011.

Notes

SUGGESTED CURRICULUM OVERVIEW

Now that we have covered just an overview of sound pedagogy, proven over the last 2,000 years, let's look at how a curriculum might be structured. After all, a teacher must have something to teach. The following example is by no means meant to be definitive, and it is not meant to be absolute; it is just a framework that can be used in total or as a base.

First and foremost, parents must avoid textbooks which have been subject to over-simplification, historical revisionism, and an obsessive focus on real and imaginary problems of Christianity and the American society. In all grades, a special emphasis must be placed on theology and doctrine, and the development of western civilization and American liberty.

The liberal arts are the great ideas that shape our culture, and preserve the very best that has ever been thought, said, or accomplished throughout history. Predominately found in writings, the liberal arts also include other artistic works such as music and painting—great works that have contributed to the development and growth of society.

The ultimate goal of a liberal arts education is knowledge, skill and wisdom—an understanding of how to live a life that is distinguished by integrity, character, charity, civility, discipline, excellence, industry and thrift, service, loyalty, originality and creativity, patriotism, and living life with a knowledge of destiny in light of the character and nature of God. The best approach to gaining a liberal arts education is through exposure to the great men and women who have promoted these ideas throughout the centuries. This cannot be effectively done through a textbook.

To learn from Moses, Solomon, Job, Mark, Luke, Paul, Aristotle, Plato, Locke, Jefferson, Hamilton, Madison, and others, one must read their works, follow their line of reasoning, study their great debates, and experience with them their struggles and their triumphs.

A liberal arts education does not differentiate learning by subject; rather, it is based on the philosophy that the mastery of one subject is incomplete without the mastery of others. Therefore, while students are learning American history, they should study the literature, as well as the scientific and mathematical discoveries of the same era. This enables the student to trace the development of ideas through history, discovering how they impacted all areas of study and shaped the development of civilization. Liberal arts students also master the skills necessary for personal and civil freedom gained through scholarship and application. Parents and teachers should focus on six specific skills: reading, writing, computation, communicating, thinking, and personal skills. Just as we do not separate subjects of study, we do not discriminate where skills should be practiced. For example, the skill of computation includes the ability to solve problems and justify (proof). These are not reserved for math and science alone, but are essential for evaluating history or writing an essay. In like manner, reading is just as important for understanding mathematics as it is for literature.

Education is more than the assimilation of facts. Proficiency in a discipline means the learner becomes a capable practitioner and has a sufficient foundation to pursue advanced study. Parents and teachers should emphasize both the acquisition and application of knowledge for the use and understanding of other foreign subjects.

The subjects that make up the curriculum are listed and briefly discussed in the next two chapters. Traditional core curriculum areas—language, history, mathematics, and science—should be strongly emphasized. The core curriculum should be enhanced with a second language and the fine arts.

Notes

PRIMARY GRADES

Language

Students should study language and literature through reading aloud, grammar and mechanics, penmanship, vocabulary, spelling instruction, and intensive phonics instruction.

Reading to others is an enduring feature of the traditional American family. All parents should pursue this tradition with their children and, so, deepen the enjoyment and reward of sharing significant literature through effective oral interpretation. Children of all ages delight in well-read stories, and this modeling by the parent provides children an excellent opportunity to experience pleasure through reading. By developing this association, students are better prepared to master the more demanding reading of the secondary years.

Parents should teach fiction and historical literature from the Western canon because they offer students models of human virtue. Through them, children become intimately acquainted with men and women of outstanding character. Children mature spiritually, intellectually, and socially from such opportunities. The growing child gains inestimable benefits from sharing in the lives of others by reading literature replete with acts of heroism, compassion, self-discipline, and faith.

When teaching literature, parents' attention should be devoted to matters of literary convention as well as to deepening the students' appreciation of the relationship between good writing and the literary character's development of virtue. By carefully considering the unfamiliar words in each book, parents assist every child's developing vocabulary. A growing ability to use language with power and grace is one of the surest marks of educated men and women and one of the surest safeguards against the loss of liberty.

Independent reading should consist of works that may be given to your child for independent reading or individual instruction. It should extend the range of your resources and contain virtuous historical and fictional depictions that most children find entertaining. It is very important you use the original unabridged versions, for most contemporary editions contain revisionist forewords and introductions that substantially undermine the literature's pedagogical value when read by impressionable children unequipped to recognize and discount the politicization of literary scholarship. Parents must examine such addenda with great care and, when in doubt, refrain from assigning them. It should go without saying *Diary of a Wimpy Kid, Harry Potter* series, and See Dick Run does not rise to this category.

Latin

For nearly two thousand years, the study of Latin has taught students grammar, vocabulary, careful reading, and precise writing. Beyond the classroom, Latin has transmitted western civilization's greatest achievements in literature, philosophy, theology, and science. Furthermore, Latin encourages good intellectual habits: students must learn to memorize information, to use systems to organize this information, and to access those systems of information smoothly. Latin has two primary goals: to expand students' understanding of language and to expose them to the Greco-Roman intellectual tradition.[171]

---

[171] For an extensive treatment of the value of Latin within a classical curriculum, see Tracy L. Simmons. *Climbing Parnassus: A New Apologia For Greek and Latin.* (Wilmington, DE: ISI Books, 2002). For the reason to begin Latin in middle school, see K. Robinson. "Why Latin in the Middle Schools?" (2007). Accessed July 6, 2008 from http://www.promotelatin.org/latinmiddle.htm.

An additional reason for learning Latin is that Latin cuts down the labor and pain of learning almost any other subject by at least 50%. It is the key to the vocabulary and structure of all Teutonic languages, as well as the technical vocabulary of all the sciences into the literature of the entire Mediterranean civilization, together with all its historical documents.

Furthermore, in order to gain a competent grasp of grammar, one needs to study a language other than English for English is uninflected and therefore too analytical and abstract to be handled effectively (as evident by most college freshmen are reading at a 7th grade level[172]) without previous practice in Dialectic.

Moreover, Latin is an inflected language and is the best language to use because it makes the study of grammar concrete and because of the historic ties of Latin to our own language and culture. Moreover, it is the ability of Latin to teach students how to think that is the most underrated of its benefits. A grammar-based Latin study is not simply a grammatical study, but an exercise what modern educators like to call "critical thinking skills." Clearly Latin is not a dead language as so many have erroneously repeated from others, but alive and breathing whether we recognize it or not.

---

[172] Andrew Clements; Christine King Farris; & Phyllis Reynolds Naylor. *What Kids Are Reading: And Why It Matters.* (Wisconsin Rapids, WI: Renaissance Reading, 2014), p. 42. Accessed January 15, 2015 from http://doc.renlearn.com/KMNet/R004101202GH426A.pdf. See Maddie Lit. "The Average College Freshman Reads At 7th Grade Level."*Campus Reform.* Leadership Institute: Arlington, VA, January 6, 2015. Assessed January 15, 2015 from http://campusreform.org/?ID=6174 & Sandra Stotsky. *Losing Our Language: How Multicultural Classroom Instruction Is Undermining Our Children's Ability to Read, Write, and Reason.* Free Press: New York, 1999.

During grades 3-6, students should focus on learning vocabulary that will assist in increasing vocabulary comprehension and usages in both English and Latin languages. Students will draw upon this new vocabulary later as they progress in their former Latin studies. Latin should be incorporated in the language program for grades 3-5. Formal Latin instruction can begin in the sixth grade. This vocabulary list does not have to be an addition to the spelling list or vocabulary but one-in-the-same.

During grades 7-8, students should focus on the basic grammar of Latin: they learn to memorize and to think systematically. They learn grammar and basic translation skills, and they begin to explore philosophy through an introduction to the pre-Socratic philosophers—Plato and Aristotle.[173]

History

The American history curriculum should strive to provide thorough coverage of American history from earliest times, to identify the major themes in America's history, and to convey a sense of the breadth of experiences and influences that have shaped the United States of America. Particular attention must be given to the role of providence in America's history and western civilization within God's creation-fall-redemption plan.

In the primary grades, the history curriculum focuses on the role of famous individuals in shaping the United States students should learn the historical significance of America's founders, statesmen, presidents, pioneers, military and religious leaders, inventors, scientists, philanthropists,

---

[173] Students begin to study Greek philosophy first for the great Christian writers had their foundation in Greek philosophy and for students to join in the Great Conversation, students must begin at the beginning of the discussion, not in the middle of it. At all times, it is imperative students assess the Great Conversation from a biblical world view and contrast the early writers and thinkers conclusions against what the Word of God has to say about the subject matter.

volunteers, and industrialists. Through biographies, autobiographies, and primary source documents, students should study American history by investigating the important contributions of the founders and the men and women who followed them.

As students study the significant contributions of famous Americans, parents and teachers portray these Americans as positive role models worthy of emulation. Values such as faith, trust, perseverance, compassion, and courage are best taught through example. The study of famous Americans provides students with countless opportunities to study the development of fine moral character.

In grades 5-8, the history curriculum should continue to focus on famous Americans and their contributions, and teachers add the element of chronological order to their history lessons.

Parents should introduce classical and biblical history early and, by grade 5, your children should begin a four-year sequence in Ancient Mesopotamian (including the Old Testament), Egyptian, Greek, Roman (including the New Testament) and medieval civilization. These courses give children the foundational knowledge needed to continue their history education at the secondary level.

Science

Biblical Christians need to become academically accomplished in science by immersion in the scientific method. Beginning in kindergarten, students should undertake simple experiments and learn the process of scientific inquiry. Each lesson should require experimentation and allow students to develop hypotheses, conduct experiments, make observations, collect data, and test the accuracy of their hypotheses. As students progress, they deepen and extend their understanding of the basic principles of sciences through a variety of scientific media and through the development of subject-appropriate vocabulary skills. Students will study Earth, life, and physical science. This will be a time to build a solid core knowledge that will be drawn upon during the high school years.

Mathematics

Students in the grammar and logic years learn numbers and operations, including numeration, basic operations, properties of numbers and operations, and estimation. They should also learn Algebra and Geometry. Additionally, students need to learn measurements and perform data analysis and probability, including data collection and representation, data set characteristics, and probability. Furthermore, students learn problem-solving skills and tools including problem-solving strategies, communication, reasoning, and proof.

Geography

Geography serves a vital function in a classical and Christian program. Five themes of geography—location, place, human interaction, movement, and regions—offer a basic approach and framework for the study of the world. Students need to learn about the complete geography of the earth and its relationship to humans. Students examine how places and countries differ, how natural and human environments work, and the connections between places, resources, people, and development. The study of geography also informs the history curriculum. So often, geographical features influence how man utilizes available resources which, in turn, affect the shaping of human history.

Christian parents and teachers should follow a pattern of concentric thinking in its geographical studies, beginning from a small central point within the community that youngest students can best appreciate, and working outward to encompass the greater land masses of regional and continental study. Under this methodology, children at the early grades study their immediate environment, including their families, school, and town. Older students study their own state geography and move on to an examination of the United States geography and other countries around the world.

It is imperative for parents to ensure that geography material aligns with the Scripture. Students must clearly understand the Genesis account of creation as the Divine fiat[174] of God before they end their logic years, for they will be equipped to examine other origins' beliefs in light of what Scripture says.

Logic

Formal logic instruction should begin in the seventh grade with in-depth study of the classical syllogism. Students should learn the four kinds of logical statements, the four ways propositions can be opposed, the three ways in which they can be equivalent, and the seven rules for the validity of syllogisms. Eighth graders should continue their formal study of logic covering the four figures of the traditional syllogism, the three forms of rhetorical arguments (called enthymemes), the three kinds of hypothetical syllogisms, the four kinds of complex syllogisms, as well as relational arguments.

Additionally, this study includes a wealth of examples of arguments from the Bible, Lewis Carroll, Isaac Watts, St. Augustine, and Tertullian, as well as extended case studies of famous arguments throughout history, such as Rene Descartes' famous enthymeme: "I think, therefore, I am"; C.S. Lewis' disjunctive syllogism proving the deity of Christ; Plato's hypothetical argument concerning the power of love; Christ's conjunctive syllogism: "You cannot serve both God

---

[174] "Divine fiat" is the creative command of God, from the Latin word *fiat*, "let there be," used by God to create the universe in the Latin version of the Book of Genesis.

and man;" David Hume's famous dilemma stating the problem of evil; the stoic Seneca's justification of the virtuous life; and St. Thomas Aquinas' cosmological argument for the existence of God.

Eighth graders should be finishing their formal study of logic by studying material logic. When most people think of logic, they think of formal logic — the study of the structure or form of reasoning. But what most educators don't realize is that formal logic is only one part of a complete logic program. The other branch of logic study was called "material logic," and focused not on the form of reasoning, but on its content.

In short, while formal logic studied the "how" of reasoning, material logic studied the "what." The principles of material logic, an important part of *trivium* language study, are now almost forgotten — a casualty of the almost exclusive modern secular emphasis on math and sciences.

Formal logic was once termed minor (or lesser) logic, while material logic usually went by the name of major (or greater) logic — a measure of how important classical thinkers considered them. Students will learn the ten ways in which something can exist, the five ways you can say something about something else, the four questions you must answer in order to know what something is, and students should perform analyses of famous essays by St. Thomas Aquinas, Hillaire Belloc, and Sir Francis Bacon.

Notes

UPPER GRADES

Humane Letters: Grades 9-12 (History and Literature).

Christian parents and teachers must maintain an unwavering commitment to the enduring principles of Christian western civilization. Careful study of the history and great literature of the West is at the core of a classical and Christian high school curriculum. Each student in grades 9-12 should take four years of rigorous coursework in western history and literature. Called the Humane Letters curriculum, this course of study offers concurrent and coordinated history and literature classes.

The Humane Letters' sequence begins in the ninth grade with an analysis of the foundation of western civilization history and literature. In the tenth grade, the study continues with a survey of medieval and early modern European history and literature. The eleventh grade examination of American history and literature leads into a twelfth grade course in American civics and economics. All through the course, particular attention must be given to the chain of Christianity and the providence of God.

The phrase, *Virtus et Sapientia* (Virtue and Wisdom), encapsulates the idea that the moral and intellectual virtues go together. They are wed, like liberty and learning. Education, therefore, is not about creating "values." Fleeting and flimsy, "values" are ultimately empty vessels into which educational fads may be dumped. The American Founding Fathers did not declare "values" upon which America was founded. Rather, the foundation was built on certain principles—truths that were timeless. Indeed, our Declaration of Independence insists upon the existence of "self-evident truths."

These truths are self-evident, however, only with the proper understanding of the terms in question. The task of a liberal arts education is arduous. In the Humane Letters curriculum, the teacher plays the important role of guide, eliciting reactions and leading discussion.

Humane Letters: Grade 12 (American Civics & Economics)

In this senior-year capstone course, students study the sources of our American liberty. They will see the indissoluble connection between liberal learning and liberty. As James Madison asked, "What spectacle can be more edifying or more reasonable than that of Liberty and Learning, each leaning on the other for their mutual and surest support?"[175] "Patriotism is as much a virtue as justice, and is as necessary for the support of societies as natural affection is for the support of families."[176] This 1773 statement, by the American patriot, Benjamin Rush, is an apt point of departure for the capstone course of the Humane Letters sequence.

An inquiry into the importance of American liberty and order, this course should explore the foundations of republican government. It considers the rights and responsibilities of citizenship and explores the fundamental principles of a free economy. It seeks, in sum, to instill in students the proper spirit of patriotism upon which self-government depends. Building upon the strong introduction to the American foundation that juniors receive in the eleventh grade history class, this course delves more deeply into early American political thought.

After completing their study of twentieth-century history, students should be introduced to the major principles of sound, economic thinking. The collapse of Communism in

---

[175] "Epilogue: Securing the Republic: James Madison to W. T. Barry 4 Aug. 1822." *The Founders' Constitution.* Volume 1, Chapter 18, Document 35. (The University of Chicago Press, 1987.) Accessed on July 15, 2014 from http://press-pubs.uchicago.edu/founders/documents/v1ch18s35.html.

[176] Benjamin Rush letter to His Fellow Countrymen: On Patriotism, October 20, 1773

the late twentieth century, as a result of its abject economic and moral failings, requires us to examine the nature of tyranny and totalitarianism. The study of civics and economics demands a confrontation with ideology following.

Mathematics

The study of mathematics is of primary importance in developing skills in logical and analytical thinking and in applying mathematical treatments to problem solving. The attainment of such knowledge and skills is important and necessary for further study in mathematics and in disciplines which are mathematically based, such as physics, chemistry, and engineering. Mathematical study begins in the ninth grade with a year of geometry, one of the seven traditional liberal arts.

The mathematics and science curricula should be coordinated in order to prepare the students mathematically for each stage of science study and to reinforce mathematical skills in science classes. For example, the mathematics used in tenth grade physics will have been studied in eighth grade Algebra I and in ninth grade geometry and, to some extent, concurrently with the study of Algebra II in tenth grade. The mathematics needed for eleventh grade chemistry and for twelfth grade advanced biology will have been completed by the end of the study of Algebra II in tenth grade. The astronomy/advanced physics in twelfth grade utilizes the mathematics learned in eleventh grade advanced mathematics and concurrently being learned in twelfth grade calculus.

Science

A four-year science curriculum is of significant importance to classical education. A thorough study of the hard sciences, based on conceptual understanding and experimentation, endows a student with necessary logic and reasoning skills. Further, such a science curriculum allows a student to question with greater confidence; he possesses a firm foundation from which meaningful questions arise.

Scientific study in high school should begin with biology in the ninth grade, followed by physics in the tenth, and chemistry in the eleventh. Twelfth graders could choose between advanced biology and astronomy/advanced physics.

This sequence of courses is designed so that each year simultaneously builds upon the previous years and prepares for future years. In biology, familiar examples are used to introduce concepts important to life. Physics students examine the concrete and recognizable phenomena of mechanics, gravity, heat, sound, light, electricity, magnetism, atoms, and nuclei. Chemistry students explore the interactions and relationships between atoms and molecules that account for chemical changes. The advanced biology course emphasizes the structures and functions of biological molecules in various levels of organisms, and in the astronomy/advanced physics course, students deepen their understanding of matter within and outside of Earth. Throughout all the courses, laboratory proficiency is fostered, allowing students to collate diverse concepts in a practical lab setting.

A classical and Christian science sequence differs from that of most public, private and homeschools, by offering physics as a tenth grade course rather than as a twelfth grade course. Because physics is, at its foundation, the most basic science, it provides the concepts that allow greater accessibility to chemistry and biology. One must understand the concept of atoms before approaching the periodic table, molecular structure, chemical bonds, and gas laws.

Further, the topics of an advanced biology course—such as cellular mechanics, development, and genetics—become illuminated only with a working foundation of physical and chemical interactions. Thus, the student begins with concrete phenomena, fully accessible to a young student, and then moves to conceptual explanation and analysis. This process approach lets students experience the excitement of science so they can better understand facts and concepts.

Technology

Technology should be used to support a child's natural way of learning. Parents and teachers should not get caught up with the progressive frenzy of "twenty-first century" technology and lose focus by keeping up with the newest widget.

Latin

Ultimately, all students should be able to translate simple Latin, on the level of Caesar's prose, and those who are able should be challenged to read Virgil. Whether students are able to read Virgil easily or with great difficulty by the end of their fourth year, however, should not solely determine success or failure in their study of Latin.

Grade 9 should begin reading abridged, unadapted Latin from Livy. Through reading the *Aeneid* and the *Odyssey*, they begin to think about the epic, the moral and spiritual virtues of the ancient world, and they become familiar with two of the foundational works in the Western canon.

In Latin grades 10 and 11, students learn to read Latin prose through Cicero, Latin poetry, and Ovid. For those who struggle with Latin, translation work is supplemented by wide readings in translation: Cicero's philosophical works, *Augustine's Confessions*, and C.S. Lewis' *Four Loves*. Grade 12 should be devoted to the *Aeneid*.

Rhetoric

The study and use of rhetorical skills have often been misunderstood as a game of words. After all, politicians, pundits and demagogues are frequently known to use "rhetoric" to obscure truth or to trick an audience into accepting a spurious argument. Such a misrepresentation is unfortunate in a world that is in need of the logic and skills of communication that can be obtained through a close study of rhetoric.

Indeed, this course of study ought to be understood as a culmination of a student's education, for in the study of rhetoric, grammar and writing, the student is taught to draw upon his now substantial body of knowledge in the creation of confident, well-reasoned and orderly arguments, expository essays, narratives, epistolary essays and poetry, as well as all manner of written and oral communication.[177]

With these tools in hand, the student can then easily decipher the spurious argument and counter with a clear, concise response. The student who has established strong convictions rooted in a worthy classical and Christian education can now effectively communicate that knowledge and those convictions in such a way as to persuade. With these skills, the student becomes a stronger citizen, able to argue on behalf of those ideals necessary for a free and moral society.

The introduction of the formal study of rhetoric should commence in the ninth grade and end in the junior year. The study of rhetoric is designed to train students in the rules, language, and art of communication. The foundations for the study of rhetoric have already been laid in their middle school studies, particularly in the study of grammar, writing, and vocabulary. In addition to these foundations, each student should be expected to present at least two memorized recitations during each academic year in order to strengthen his skills in memorization as well as his experience in public presentation.

The high school study of rhetoric is, therefore, neither completely foreign nor is it entirely novel. It is also not purely oral in its emphasis, but incorporates written argument as well. What is new to the student is the introduction of formal

---

[177] Susan Wise Bauer & Jessie Wise. *The Well-Trained Mind: A Guide To Classical Education At Home* (Rev. and updated ed.). (New York: W.W. Norton & Co., 2004).

rules and types of communication central to the study of rhetoric.

Physical Education

As part of the classical and Christian education tradition, educating the mind is incomplete without educating the body as well. As Plato writes, physical education "should produce health, agility, and beauty in the limbs and parts of the body, giving the proper reflection and extension to each of them."[178]

---

[178] Plato, *The Laws, Book VII.*

Notes

Coming Home

The idea of a university, a point in which all things come together, is inescapably biblical. The idea of university presupposes as Paul says, "one Lord, one faith, one baptism, one God and Father of all who is above all and through all and in you all."[179] If you have such an article of faith, you have a universe, and you can have a university because truth is God-given, and it is one of the same in every sphere.

That is to say truth is one and the same in inner space, in every atom of our being, and in outer space, because the same God made all things, and His stamp is unmistakably in every atom, every fiber of all creation. This means there is a unified field of knowledge, that all truths is interrelated because it comes from the hand of one creator, there is a universe, and there can be a university and there can be the kind of education you and I believe in, because there is the God of scripture which is the only source of truth we can completely be sure of.

---

[179] Eph 4:6 & 1 Cor. 8:6

Biblical Worldview of the Christian Life and Christian Education

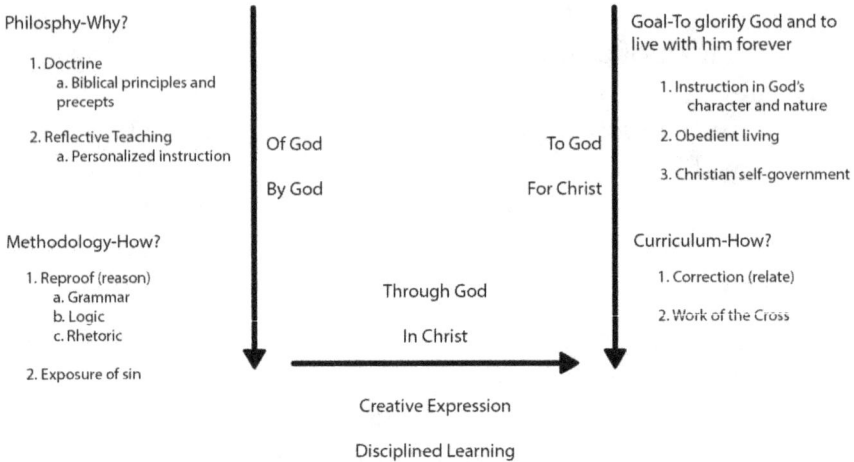

Philosphy-Why?

1. Doctrine
   a. Biblical principles and precepts

2. Reflective Teaching
   a. Personalized instruction

Methodology-How?

1. Reproof (reason)
   a. Grammar
   b. Logic
   c. Rhetoric

2. Exposure of sin

Of God

By God

Through God

In Christ

To God

For Christ

Goal-To glorify God and to live with him forever

1. Instruction in God's character and nature

2. Obedient living

3. Christian self-government

Curriculum-How?

1. Correction (relate)

2. Work of the Cross

Creative Expression

Disciplined Learning

To deny this faith and the university, as it has historically existed, results moral in educational anarchy. Basic to education, therefore, is the fact that by Him all things were made, and without him was nothing was made; this is the key to learning.

Education must be God-centered. Henry Van Til some years ago in his book: *Christianity and Culture*, said that culture is religion externalized, it is a faith applied to the world. In so defining culture, Henry Van Til was simply stating what was an obvious fact, what men had known for untold generations. But what we see now is a redefinition of all things, in order to destroy their meanings, in order to eliminate our faith.[180]

---

[180] Cited in R.J. Rushdoony. "Education As A Religious Discipline, part 1." (Lecture Transcript, n.d.) Retrieved December 1, 2014 from http://www.pocketcollege.com/transcripts/FinishedHTML/021%20-%20Education%20as%20a%20Religious%20Discipline%20-%20Aaron/RR173A1%20-%20Education%20as%20a%20Religious%20Discipline.html.

But with secularism, there is no possibility of university. In fact, everything is possible other than the One True God of the Bible. Those who hold to the worldview of secularism, agree almost anything could exist. But the one thing that could not exist is an overarching rule of law, an overarching God, an order that is the same everywhere, one Lord, one faith, one universe.

Those who control every aspect of our education system, in by in large both private and homeschool, through the curriculum designs and pedagogy is ready to admit the possibility of any kind of truth. Except that which we as bible believing Christians believe, that which God set forth in His infallible word. As a result, the education system is open to anything except our faith. It includes occultism, Islam, Buddhism, and everything else in the curriculum, but not the scripture.

Education is inescapably religious. Ultimately we have only two kinds of education humanistic, in terms of Genesis 3:5 every man is his own god, and Christian, in terms of scripture, in terms of the triune God as the ultimate authority. There can be no halting, no indecision as we face the alternative. If we make the wrong choice, God will be no more favorable to us than he was to the compromisers of old who compromised with Baal and Baal worship.

Biblical Approach to Theocentric Education

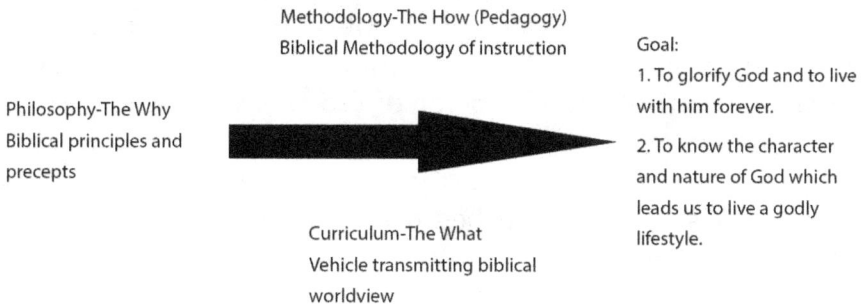

Methodology-The How (Pedagogy)
Biblical Methodology of instruction

Goal:
1. To glorify God and to live with him forever.

Philosophy-The Why
Biblical principles and precepts

2. To know the character and nature of God which leads us to live a godly lifestyle.

Curriculum-The What
Vehicle transmitting biblical worldview

Education is a religious discipline; our choice of education tells us who our lord is. Our choice of schooling we give our children reveals whether our Lord is the God of Abraham Isaac and Jacob, whether it is the Lord Jesus Christ that we serve or whether it is man.

In the Bible, education is inseparable from the fact that man is created in the image of God. And the image of God is defined for us in different passages of scripture as knowledge, righteousness, justice, holiness, and dominion; and each of these aspects is basic to education.

For Christians, the purpose of education is to gain knowledge in order that we might better serve God, righteousness or justice that we might know and apply the law of God to every sphere. That we dedicate ourselves to God in all that we are, our families, our possessions and that we might acknowledge Christ asking in every sphere of life and thought.

Christian education rests on the premise that man is created in the image of God. Humanistic education rests on the premise that man is a creature who is a product of evolution, a blind chance, and, as a result, is the sole voice of reason in an unreasoning and absurd creation.

If we are going to have a Christian life and worldview, the first thing, we are going to have to have, is a Christian God view. How we think about God will determine how we think about the world and how we think about our lives. I really don't think the Christian community, in general, devotes much thought of the character of God. And I hear over and over, "I don't need to know any theology, all, I need to know, is Jesus." That is all fine and good and all, but who is Jesus anyway? As soon as you begin to answer this question, you have just plunged yourself into theology.

The Christian life and worldview seeks to establish the rules of thinking, the rules for determining how we know what is true. Who is telling the truth, how do you know? That is a question of epistemology. Ultimately, what is the truth—what is it, is it real ultimately. That is a metaphysical question. Who is the truth is a theological question. How does the truth relate to me is an anthropological question. And how the truth commands me is an ethical question. These are the elements of a Christian life in worldview.

It is my hope that this short book has served to help explain some of the things you may have sensed have been going on in our world today; in particular the influences permeating our schools, books, and entertainment. Furthermore, for those who have provided your children a clearly distinctive and biblically based education, I hope I have assisted in your conviction in continuing to do so.

When you stop and think about the worldviews that surround us; I hope you will hear the voice of Paul of Tarsus in the wind, "Take every thought captive." He is reminding us, as believers; we are not from this time and space. We are not to conform to the ways of this world. Furthermore, it is my hope that I have been able to assist you in developing a biblical conviction for providing a theocentric education and schooling for your children. Additionally, I hope I have provided information that you can act upon when evaluating curriculum or the educational institution you may be considering for your children.

Soli deo Gloria!

For additional information concerning the American education system and homeschooling from a biblical worldview and additional resources, visit **www.edstruggle.com**.

Isaac Moffett is the host of the weekly podcast and blog, The Great Education Struggle, which addresses the American education system and homeschooling from a biblical worldview.

Isaac has taught in public school for eight years and has served as a private school administrator. He has earned a Master's of Science in Educational Leadership, Post-BA Secondary Teacher Certification in History and Social Studies and a Bachelors of Arts in Social and Behavioral Science.

Isaac has been featured on numerous programs and publications including being interviewed by Robert F. Kennedy's youngest son, Douglas Kennedy of Fox News Channel. Isaac lives in Nampa, Idaho with his wife Tracy, his three daughters and one son.